ADVANCE PRAISE

"A guide for writers who welcome the dark and hunger for meaning. Part craft, part devotion, *Writing at the Wellspring* is a call to surrender control, listen beneath the noise, and create from the place where awe and fear meet. If the page is a threshold, this book will show you how to cross." — Joanna Penn, author of *Writing the Shadow*

"I can't think of any [books] that link the creative act so uniquely or perrsuasively with spirituality — more specifically with the weird and uncanny as well as the life path of personal awakening — as Matt Cardin's *Writing at the Wellspring*." — Victoria Nelson, author of *On Writer's Block* and *The Secret Life of Puppets*

"The most illuminating book on creativity I've read in a long time. I consider it the third essential tome in a 'trilogy of creativity,' made up of *The Artist's Way* by Julia Cameron, *The War of Art* by Steven Pressfield, and now *Writing at the Wellspring* by Matt Cardin." — Clint Watson, founder of BoldBrush

"[A]t once a spur to literary expression and a meditation on the silence and darkness out of which all creative acts emerge, and to which they all return. A guide for writers unlike any other." — J. F. Martel, author of *Reclaiming Art in the Age of Artifice* and co-host of *Weird Studies*

"If you're seeking permission to trust the dark unknown that guides your work, and your way of being in the world, this book offers profound companionship on that journey." — Amanda Saint, author, publisher, and founder of The Mindful Writer

"This book's understanding of no-self makes it especially important to any writer ready to see through the self illusion and realize the freedom this brings to any creative work. It lovingly deconstructs what our culture believes — what you believe — about how writing happens." — Katrijn van Oudheusden, author of *Seeing No Self: Essential Questions to Reveal Our Nondual Nature*

EARLY READER REACTIONS

"[A] gift to anyone with a core creative longing." — Annalise Oatman, artist/ psychotherapist

"I went through a challenging relationship with my writing, and your voice is helping me find my way out of that particular dark." — M. Rickert, World Fantasy Award-winning author of *Map of Dreams*

"You're writing some of the freshest stuff on spiritual creativity I've seen since Julia Cameron and Natalie Goldberg." — R. J.

"Thank you for reconnecting me to a piece of myself that was buried just beneath the surface of the words I was writing. Engaging consciously with my daimon muse is the magic I needed." — Kaleiheana Stormcrow, writer/dreamer

"From my perspective, this work is part of the essential work, the necessary 'remembering,' the deep river of wisdom that is flowing from a true source." — Carl Austin Hyatt, award-winning photographer

"I just want to say that what you're doing feels revolutionary in this historical moment, getting us to focus on the voice within. It's the only thing that can possibly save this species."— Keiko Ohnuma, writer/journalist

"Invaluable and sometimes eerily serendipitous — the perfect book for this moment in my life." — Christian Farrell, artist/educator

"It has been a tremendous help in shifting how I see creativity and ultimately life itself." — Jonathan Blake, artist

"This is a league apart from other books on creativity.... I can't imagine anyone reading this book being the same person at the end as they were at the beginning." — Melanie Leavey, author/artist

Writing
at the
Wellspring

Tapping the Source of
Your Inner Genius

Matt Cardin

DEEP CURRENT PRESS

PYATT · ARKANSAS

ISBN: 979-8-9932097-0-8

LIBRARY OF CONGRESS CONTROL NUMBER:
2025921584

DESIGN, TYPOGRAPHY,
PROJECT MANAGEMENT & PRODUCTION
D. Patrick Miller, Fearless Literary
www.fearlessbooks.com/Literary.html

TABLE OF CONTENTS

PREFACE 1

INTRODUCTION: *On Writing and Living into the Dark* 5

PART ONE: THE CALL OF THE DAEMON 23

1: *The Hidden River of Your Writing* 25

2: *The Daemon of Pen and Page* 35

3: *The Daemon in Exile: A Cultural History* 45

4: *Meet Your Inner Genius* 57

5: *To Thine Own Muse Be True* 77

6: *The Writer's Paradox* 91

7: *Invite the Lightning* 97

8: *Embrace The Unknown* 109

PART TWO: THE FLASHPOINT OF SILENCE 115

9: *Surrender to Stillness* 117

10: *The Crossroads of Spirit and Art* 133

11: *Nonduality and the Daemon* 143

12: *Breaking the Spell of Words* 149

PART THREE: THE AXIS OF CREATION 161

13: *The Illusion of Obstruction* 163

14: *The Flow of Creation* 171

15: *The Teleology of Now* 189

16: *Creative Purpose in a Collapsing World* 205

BIBLIOGRAPHY.. 225

INDEX.. 231

ACKNOWLEDGMENTS................................. 239

ABOUT THE AUTHOR.................................. 241

ALSO BY MATT CARDIN 243

PREFACE

IN ONE WAY or another, every book reflects its author's personal experience. This is certainly true of all the books I have written, including not only my collections of stories and essays exploring the intersection of spirituality and religion with metaphysical and ontological horror, but also the three encyclopedias that I have edited and curated (on mummies, the paranormal, and the history of horror literature). Whether I'm writing fiction or nonfiction, and whether I'm working on my own writing or helping to birth a collective work through editorial shaping and visioning, it's all connected to my core creative fascination. And I know the same is true of you and your writing.

For me, the deeply personal nature of all this is especially pronounced when I write about creativity itself, particularly in relation to spiritual insight or awakening. This was the focus of my previous book on the subject, *A Course in Demonic Creativity*, and it is likewise the focus here. *Writing at the Wellspring* takes it in a fresh direction, not by choice, but because this is simply where my understanding and engagement with the topic have led. This is no different from what happens to all of us when we're creating honestly, from the center of our authentic perception and motivation. But sometimes the quality of personalness is more explicitly visible on the surface of a given work. That's definitely the case here.

And that's why I think this book will speak most directly to readers who share not only my topical interests but a sympathetic sensibility. I have never been able to reduce my native fascinations to a single focus, and virtually the entire gamut of what moves me, not only now but over the decades, is reflected in one way or another in the pages that follow. So, I thought I would take a moment in this preface to specify who the book is for, based on who I believe will feel most at home in it because they grok the same things that I do when considering the heady themes of inspiration, insight, and the writer's path.

This book will most likely appeal to you if you find yourself reflected in any or all of the following:

- You feel that true creativity, more than just skill or self-expression, requires listening to something deeper.
- You long to create in a way that feels honest, awake, and aligned with your truest self.
- You struggle with resistance not just as a block to productivity, but as a spiritual and psychological threshold.
- You find yourself drawn to nonduality, inner stillness, or mystical insight, not as abstract philosophy but as vivid recognition.
- You've glimpsed the uncanny truth that inspiration may not be yours but something that comes through you.
- You resonate with the idea of the muse or daemon, an inner presence that guides, haunts, and transforms your work.
- You see the signs of cultural unraveling and feel called to respond not with more noise, but with depth.

- You sometimes feel becalmed, both creatively and existentially, and find this confusing or even distressing.
- You hunger for the kind of writing that fuses the spiritual and the strange, even verging into the shadow realm of the weird, the ominous, and the numinous.
- You enjoy exploring the inner lives of other writers and seekers, and learning how they have grappled with the creative mystery.
- You sense, perhaps dimly, that your creative path is inseparable from your path of awakening, and that both are leading you somewhere beyond yourself.

For further orientation and grounding, here's a quick road map:

In this book's introduction, I explore the strange convergence of personal inspiration and collective cultural crisis, introducing the core concept of living into the dark and proposing that our creative blocks and breakthroughs are bound up with more profound questions of identity, meaning, and metaphysical truth.

Part One, *The Call of the Daemon*, explores the mysterious nature of inspiration and the deeper forces — psychological, spiritual, and perhaps transpersonal — that shape the creative act. It lays out a view of creativity as a collaboration with a semi-autonomous inner intelligence rather than a product of conscious effort, and it examines this muse or daemon as inner companion, creative double, and emissary of something beyond the ego. It also looks at how this figure was ejected from mainstream Western intellectual culture, with harrowing consequences that still shape us today.

Part Two, *The Flashpoint of Silence*, turns to the role of spiritual stillness in authentic creativity. It investigates how silence, surrender, and the collapse of self-as-doer are often preconditions for creative emergence. It also considers the uncomfortable tension that we can sometimes feel between our creative and spiritual motivations.

Part Three, *The Axis of Creation*, brings these threads together in an exploration of resistance, creative flow, and the act of writing as a spiritual path. It intensely interrogates and deconstructs the experience of creative block, and it considers how creative practice, when aligned with one's deeper nature, can become not just a source of personal insight but a sustaining way of being in a time of cultural upheaval. The final chapter presents creativity as a way to preserve meaning and consciousness in a decaying culture by fulfilling one's unique purpose. It reimagines creative-spiritual practice as a form of quiet devotion, a grounded, even monastic, orientation to life in a disoriented world.

Again, if any of this resonates or connects, this book is probably for you. We're most likely kindred spirits, so maybe some of what I share here will resonate and help you along your creative path, until it becomes evident that there's really no path at all, no journey or destination, but just a timeless presence, absolutely here and inescapably now, where creation is continuously unfolding in the very fact of your own being, which takes the appearance of a self and a world, and which sometimes takes the form of writing or creating other things within that dream. I'm glad we found each other in this world of shifting shadows.

On Writing and Living into the Dark

If a man wishes to be sure of the road he treads on,
he must close his eyes and walk in the dark.
— ST. JOHN OF THE CROSS (attrib.)

FOUR YEARS AGO, on a warm August morning in the North Arkansas Ozarks, I found myself standing on stage in front of a couple hundred colleagues — faculty, advisors, deans, fellow administrators, my boss (the president) — giving a convocation address to kick off the academic year at the college where I serve as vice president of academic affairs. My theme was creativity, purpose, and the road ahead, as part of a keynote where I was discussing Simon Sinek's famous concept of "finding your why." In the process of personalizing it, I found my mostly extemporaneous words turning toward the topic of long-term future goals and how I have always been constitutionally incapable of establishing them.

This brought to mind my most recent employee performance review. At my college, the HR-provided form for writing that annual document contains a question asking employees to reflect on where they want to be, career-wise, five years into the future. It also asks how we plan to get there.

In real time, as I was addressing my colleagues, I realized that what I had written in my last performance review was germane to my chosen topic. So I quoted from it. And now I quote from it again, here, to you, as a way to explain our point of departure in this book as we meld our separate minds together through the medium of the printed word and head into an intense consideration of writing and creativity in the context of spiritual awakening and the daemon muse:

> This is always a question that makes me sound like a distinctly unmotivated person when I try to answer it, because I have no five-year goals. All the best things that have happened in my life, career-wise and otherwise, have been the result of serendipity as I have made a point of living in the present and following the path that presents itself right now. Life knows what it wants from me. Five years from now, I'll find out what I'm supposed to be doing five years from now. If I have any plan for reaching that, it's simply to concentrate wholly on this moment, the here and now, and fulfill what it asks of me, in the confidence that this will lead organically and inevitably to what is supposed to be in the future.

If I now tell you that what I said there also describes the way I write, perhaps you won't find this surprising. But I will say it anyway, for it serves as fair warning that the chapters that follow are doing their own thing and going their own way under their own power. When I wrote them as essays at separate moments in time, and even when I realized they wanted to be assembled into this book, and even as I was organizing and editing them into a manuscript and working to intuit and elicit a through line, I was really just following along. Kind of like you are now.

This overall approach and attitude is what I have come to think of as *living into the dark*, though I did not share that phrase with my colleagues at that fall convocation. It first came to me in association with another, related phrase: *writing into the dark*. But that one isn't original to me. It came from someone else.

On Writing Into the Dark

That someone is Dean Wesley Smith, the prolific science fiction, fantasy, and mystery novelist. In the spring and summer of 2019 when I was finishing up my Ph.D. at the same time that my twenty-year collection of supernatural horror fiction, *To Rouse Leviathan* (featuring two stories co-written with the redoubtable Mark McLaughlin), was about to be published, I found myself reflecting on my writing career, my future in academia, and my life's general direction. I was also doing a lot of meditating and spiritual reading. I had long been a proponent of something like divine guidance, particularly via the experience of communing with and listening to the inner genius or daemon muse, which we will explore in this book. And I was strongly intuiting the parallels and overlaps between this approach to both creative artistic work and life at large. As I tried to express the matter to myself, I found words and phrases like "blind guidance" and "walking forward into the darkness" coalescing in my mind.

Being a long-time initiate into life's School of Synchronicities, and knowing that strange and striking coincidences tend to occur around times of transition and intensified inner energy, I should have recognized that I was in precisely that fertile state of mind and soul in which the inner and outer worlds tend to spontaneously, meaningfully align. But this did not prevent me from feeling a jolt of genuine surprise when, a few months into this period of creative and philosophical ferment, an Internet search whose terms I have long since forgotten yielded the phrase "writing into the dark." And it wasn't just a phrase. It was the title of a book. The author was Dean Wesley Smith. After investigating it for about thirty seconds, I knew I had to read it.

Smith's thesis in *Writing into the Dark* is that novelists can dispense with long-range planning and instead rely on their creative mind to envision a complete story and produce a book. He says that, contrary to widespread opinion, an outline is not necessary. You can simply start writing, establish the story's initial circumstances, and from there continue to write from the edge of the developing narrative moment, trusting that what happens next will emerge naturally. Yes, there's a bit more to it than that. Smith develops his idea with additional — and quite savvy and useful — advice about such things as "creative cycling," what to do if you get stuck, and how to create a "reverse outline" by looking back over the latest section of a draft and making notes about the pattern it reveals, which can then spur you forward into the next part. Still, in essence, his overall counsel really is that simple: Trust your creative mind. Abandon the attempt to plan things ahead of time. Let the vision emerge as you write. Write into the dark.

In late 2019 when I absorbed all of this, it resonated so perfectly with what I was thinking and feeling that I knew I was really onto something. I recognized that I was in the familiar position of being deeply influenced by seeing/hearing someone else skillfully articulate what I was already trying to state for myself.

In addition to purchasing and reading Smith's book, I eagerly tracked down and read many articles and blog posts about it, some by Smith himself. I also watched several videos, including a recording of an excellent talk that Smith gave at a conference in Las Vegas where he outlined the entire approach.

Then I came across another video, and this is what made the full connection to my larger set of concerns. Like I have said, the idea of proceeding without knowledge, without a preconceived plan, is broader than just the question of writing and creative artistic work. It expands to encompass life as a whole, linking writing to the world. So that's why this next video, which I encountered right as I was digesting and appreciating Smith's advice, drove home the impact of his core concept even more deeply.

The video features fantasy and horror novelist Michael La Ronn on his "Author Level Up" YouTube channel explaining how *Writing into the Dark* was "the foundational book that changed everything" for him. He says his adoption of Smith's approach marked a turning point in his writing career, helping him not only to write with greater speed and volume, but to write better by producing more compelling and fully realized novels.

At one point La Ronn offers an effective summary of Smith's advice on trusting the creative mind, what Smith calls the creative voice: "Creativity comes from the back of the brain.... Others might call it a muse or your subconscious."

La Ronn points out that Smith contrasts the creative voice with the critical voice, which comes from the front of the brain and has the job of keeping you safe. Outlining is an activity we perform with the critical voice. Since that voice's job is to protect you, it tends to stomp all over its tender, sensitive sibling, heaping criticisms on its spontaneous attempts at storytelling, which represent vulnerability and therefore feel dangerous to the self. Hence, the wisdom of working without an outline, of writing into the dark, which sidesteps the critical voice and lets the creative voice speak freely.

La Ronn identifies the following passage in Smith's book as his favorite:

> [W]riting into the dark takes a belief system in story. It takes a trust that your creative voice knows what it is doing. And it takes a vast amount of mental fight to walk against all the myths and let the fine work your creative voice has done alone and not ruin it with your critical voice.[1]

Like La Ronn, I appreciate this passage. And being who I am, even as I listened to La Ronn talk about it, I had already begun to brood on the wider, life-level applications of embracing this attitude of trust toward one's deep creative core — something I had previously written about in *A Course in Demonic Creativity: A Writer's Guide to the Inner Genius* — when La Ronn took a turn into this very thing and dramatically broadened the scope of Smith's advice:

> Writing as a belief system. That got me thinking about my relationship with religion. I believe in a higher power. I can't prove it, though. For example, I could tell you about an emotional experience I had that gives me faith, but you

can't see it. I can't really convince you that a God exists. Yet I still choose to have my own belief system because of faith. Faith is believing in something even if you can't see it, even if you can't prove it. Without faith, you don't have a belief system. It's the cornerstone on which any belief on anything intangible rests.

I'm going to get philosophical for a minute, but for me, writing is sacred. It's as sacred as prayer. When I sit down and write, and simply trust my creative voice and have full faith in it, I'm connecting with something higher than myself, for reasons beyond myself. Because I don't outline, I never know where my story is going to go, but I trust my creative voice. And it always, always, always comes through for me. It has not failed me, not even once. But that, like belief in any major religion, takes an incredible amount of faith.[2]

Borrowing a metaphor from Smith, La Ronn compares the experience of using this intuitive approach to write a book — or, potentially, to do anything else — to entering a deep, dark cave without knowing where the exit lies. It's dark. It's frightening. You can sense unseen shapes in the gloom that envelops you. A feeling of dread arises. But eventually, if you continue crawling through the darkness with faith that a hidden intelligence is guiding and accompanying you, you will emerge into the sunlight on the other side, filled with a euphoric sense of freedom and fulfillment. And the story of your journey through the cave will be rich and rewarding to share.

Like I said, when I encountered all of this, it dovetailed perfectly and powerfully with the thoughts that were already percolating within me about trusting intuitive inner guidance. So it's surely no surprise that right then, back in October 2019 when I first read Dean Wesley Smith's book and watched Michael La Ronn's video, my thoughts seized upon the idea of "writing into the dark" and modified it to "living into the dark." I have been using it ever since as an accurate and straightforward description of what I, as this notional separate identity that I call "Matt," am really doing at any given moment of the day, night, week, month, or year, no matter what object-oriented or goal-oriented activities I may otherwise seem to be involved in on the surface.

It's a point so central, so crucial, not only to me but to you, and also to the anti-outline (as it were) of this book, that I want to pause on it for a moment to break down the components of the phrase itself, "living into the dark," and call out some of their implicit and embedded meanings.

On Living Into the Dark

Living into the dark means living with no plan, no rigid goals, no outline. It means foregoing the impossible attempt to plot a path to a preconceived end. It means accepting, even embracing, that the future is unknowable, that all your thoughts about it are pure projection and abstraction. Beyond even this, it means accepting that you will never actually live your way into the future, since the future only ever arrives as a kind of cloud formation in the eternal and evanescent present: always new, always unexpected, always categorically eluding and transcending your mental images of it.

On living...

This understanding and experience of life has unfolded and intensified for me over the span of my five-plus decades. The wisdom that has seemed to want to force itself upon me is that human life is a process of, first, having rigid expectations and assumptions built up about literally everything — about what people, families, and communities are like; about the solidity and givenness of familial, institutional, societal, cultural, and civilizational arrangements; about what you should expect and hope for, what brings pleasure and fulfillment, how you should view the purpose, trajectory, and meaning of your life; about your very own self, who and what you really are, and the relationship between this self and the world — and then seeing these ruthlessly deconstructed and demolished. The agent of this demolition is not a person, people, groups, or a society with some evil or spiteful agenda against you. Rather, the agent is reality itself.

Life, it seems to me, is in essence a massive head fake. From the moment you're born, it says, "Here's what I am, and here's what you are." And you, being young and naïve, run with it. You accept what it tells you. You receive its enculturation. And then at some point, life suddenly, shockingly crows "Gotcha!" and makes an impossible slam dunk at the opposite end of a playing court you didn't even know you were on, after which the walls and floor crumble away and you find yourself hurtling endlessly, weightlessly through the empty space of an infinite jeweled cosmos like the doomed astronauts spilling out of the shredded spaceship in Ray Bradbury's "Kaleidoscope." Living into the dark means living with full, acute awareness that this is all the case. It means letting this awareness suffuse and transmute your sense of everything.

In the case of a book on writing and spiritual awakening that starts with an introduction devoted to this theme, it means writing without a definite plan, assembling and editing contents as they want to be assembled in the moment, making adjustments and then meta-adjustments as they suggest themselves, leaving key redundancies intact among the individual chapters/essays instead of smoothing and editing them out, because each piece is really a different colored pane in a stained glass window refracting the same dark light, and generally letting the thing have its head and run where it will. Just like I'm doing right now.

If at this point you're still with me, I can only assume this approach speaks to you on some level.

... into the dark

I want to say something, too, about the term "dark." In this book, and in much of my writing career over the past quarter century — and in my life as a whole — "dark" carries a welter of inter-linked connotations that are in full effect here.

The dark in the evocative phrase at hand means dark as in un-seeable and unknowable, not available to perception, cognition, or direct awareness—much like the darkness of the unconscious mind, ever unknowable to the conscious ego except as a shadowy presence that always accompanies, precedes, and stands behind, looking over the ego's shoulder, as it were.

It means dark as in the darkness that, in the perennially evocative imagery of Genesis 1, "covered the face of the deep" in the primordial state of uncreated chaos before God spoke and shaped it into an ordered cosmos.

It means dark like the numinous shadows and gloom of Gothic and supernatural horror, which conceal, embody, and emanate all the heady, paradoxical potency of Rudolf Otto's *mysterium tremendum et fascinans*, the awesome divine mystery before which we tremble with helpless fascination and dread.

It means dark as in Abram's transformative encounter with Yahweh in Genesis 15: "As the sun was going down, a deep sleep fell upon Abram, and a deep and terrifying darkness descended upon him. Then God spoke to him." I have actually always been partial to the rendering of this verse in the Douay-Reihms 1899 American edition, where the divine visitation is described as "a great and darksome horror."

It means dark as in the fertile yin soil of the creative unconscious, which can manifest as the muse, the daemon, and the inner genius, not only in pretty words with overtones of mythic symbolism, but in actual firsthand experience.

It means dark like the "cloud of unknowing" that, in the words of the anonymous author of the classic fourteenth-century Christian contemplative treatise bearing that title, must always "remain between you and God" in this life, "preventing you from seeing him in the clear light of rational understanding, and from experiencing his loving sweetness in your affection." The author advises us to reconcile ourselves to waiting in this cloud, this ignorance, while continuing to long for God. "For if you are to feel him or to see him in this life, it must always be in this cloud, in this darkness."

It means dark as in the apocalyptically unsettled tenor of our present collective cultural moment in the first half of the twenty-first century of the so-called Common Era, when God, the universe, fate, the zeitgeist, name your higher power, seems hellbent on demonstrating to all of us the aforementioned emergent meta-principle of crumbling cosmos and reversed expectations.

These are some connotations of the word in question within the context of this book, my other writings, and, as I have said, our lives. Having caught the drift, you can surely articulate more of them yourself if you feel so led.

The Daemon at the End of the World

And speaking of the apocalypse, there is a question that inevitably presents itself in an age like ours to people who read and write books like this: What good are things like writing and art? Don't they stand revealed as comparatively frivolous in a world that is coming apart at the seams?

Because the world, as you have probably noticed, is flinging itself to pieces. This is the felt and lived experience of millions, even billions, around the globe in the twenty-first century. Since the turn of the millennium, and really for quite some time before that, human societies all over the planet have entered a period of intense collective crisis marked by seismic cultural convulsions of a pointedly apocalyptic cast. In such circumstances, aren't we being a little too precious, aren't we being heedless and self-absorbed, if we give attention to our little creative projects and desires? Don't bigger and more important things call for our attention instead?

In a word: no. Quite the opposite, in fact. In a world of apocalyptic breakdown and a rapidly immanentizing eschaton, creative artistic pursuits become all the more important. This is especially true right now, amid the centripetal forces that have turned contemporary life into a convincing facsimile of a dystopian dark age that threatens to smother the creative artistic impulse under the collective weight of a dying civilization. Far from being a time to abandon writing and art, this is a time to double down on them, and to seek clarity on what they are for and how they can help us.[3]

Enter the daemon, already mentioned above. At this cultural moment, the old concept of the writer's daemon, the artist's muse, the thinker's inner genius, returns with an offer to help us find and fulfill our individual and collective creative destinies in a way that is healing and constructive. To adopt the discipline of the daemon muse by relating to creative energy and calling as a separate, collaborative intelligence is to embark on a kind of monastic path, a way of life that is devoted to sheltering, nurturing, and bringing forth each person's unique gifts so that they can meet the world's specific needs at a crucial inflection point in history. Such a discipline may even enable the laying of cultural seeds that will come to fruition on the other side of the apocalypse, in some far-future renaissance. I will return to this theme and say more about it in the final chapter.

Moreover, this approach to creativity in writing, art, and life directly confronts the deep nature of the crisis itself, since one way to understand what's happening is to recognize it as the inevitable result of a collective daimon run amok and turned monstrous because of fateful decisions, reaching back to the eighteenth century and the birth of modern science and social structures, that excluded the daemon muse and the visionary powers it represents from our collective map of reality.

In sum, as the world grows weirder and more disturbed, the discipline of the daemon muse may enable us to heal that fateful rupture and find a life of meaning and purpose by fulfilling our unique callings right in the midst of a new dark age.

There Is No Grand Scheme

In these ways and others, my whole life has been an experience of living into the dark. As Thomas Ligotti once wrote in his short novel *My Work Is Not Yet Done,* "There is no grand scheme of things." Or rather, there is a grand scheme — and it's one that I, that we, can only read in reverse, never ahead or straight-on, for it is part and parcel of that numinous darkness.

So all these things, plus more, serve as the starting point for this book. Which is to say that I have no plan here, other than to remain true to my sense of guidance by personal interest, natural affinity, and inner gravitational attraction. I hope you approach these pages with the same intent. In 1981, Bill Moyers asked Dame Rebecca West to identify the mood of the present age. She paused a moment, then replied, "A desperate search for a pattern." I would argue that the same still holds true for today's collective mood, only more so. And I would argue that following your daemon muse into the darkness, trusting the given path of your unique life experience, which you can only see illumined a single step ahead — if even that far — as you walk into the shadows of the unknown, provides the only pattern, or at least the only true and sound one — as opposed to the false narratives, worldviews, and life maps that are constantly clamoring to enter our heads and hearts from the outside — that is available to you. In a profound sense, it is the only true path and pattern that any of us has ever had available.

I should add that this darkness that has decided to talk about itself so much here at the beginning — the darkness into which, as it was for Seamus Heaney, everything I know is a doorway, and into which I am now and have always been living and writing — is not always or even usually foregrounded in the pages that follow. Many other themes and interests assert themselves throughout. But it does stand perpetually and pervasively behind the scenes, moving in and as the shadows at the edges of the lit stage, leading ever onward toward that final reunion and fulfillment whose inevitability has entranced me with longing and terror since before I had those words to describe it.

I might also note that this same luminous, numinous darkness is now and always has been your own constant companion. Eventually, in some unique form suited to each of us, we all encounter it. We are all forced to acknowledge it, though we tend to tamp it down, cover it up, and deny or ignore its truth. The name we usually give to this act of repression and denial is "living my life."

My point is that we are all, in our separate ways, consciously or unconsciously, living into the dark.

Darkness and Light

And yet... and yet... beyond even that nicely poetic-sounding extremity, which is so tempting for me to leave as the last word of this introduction, there is still something further: the ultimate reversal, the ontological jiu-jitsu flip that reality employs to finally floor us. This occurs when we pass through that barrier of shadow, crawl through the dreadful cave, come out on the other side, and blink in astonishment at the blinding pure glow of what we had always — and to be fair, given our circumstances, had always inevitably — mistakenly dreaded as a fearsome darkness, when it was really the only pure light there ever has been or ever could be.

It is with that flip that I invite you to turn with me to the matter of writing, creativity, waking up, and the question of what they all have to do with each other, and of how finding out the unique answer in your own life can tell you who you really are and what you're really here to do.

Matt Cardin
Pyatt, Arkansas
August 2025

NOTES

1. Dean Wesley Smith, *Writing into the Dark: How to Write a Novel without an Outline* (WMG Publishing, 2015), 39.
2. This and the previous two quoted passages are transcribed from Michael La Ronn, "Writing into the Dark: Write a Book Without an Outline!" June 22, 2018, YouTube, 09:47, *https://youtu.be/w33JlZsVJYI?si=hiQU7rtLCeT3srPb.*
3. On this point, I can't help pausing in a footnote to recommend a truly necessary book: *Reclaiming Art in the Age of Artifice* by J. F. Martel. The book argues that art, contrary to received modern opinion, "precedes the formation of culture and even society" and "is free of politics and ideology," and thus provides a connection to a primal, transcendent reality that acts as "a force of liberation wherever it breaks through the trance of humdrum existence." Originally published in 2015 by North Atlantic Books, it was republished in a new edition by Basic Books in 2025 with a new introduction by Donna Tartt, which underscores its significance. I provided a blurb for the original edition, and I still stand by every word: "This is a fascinating and invigorating book. In explaining art as a concrete expression of a mythic reality that is simultaneously beautiful, awesome, terrifying, numinous, and sublime, J. F. Martel fuses a high metaphysical and ontological vision with a rich sensibility that

is equal parts mysticism and weird horror. What's more, he offers a dead-on diagnosis of our present cultural moment as an 'age of artifice' in which political and commercial concerns have hijacked the power of art and forced it to serve the demons of hype and propaganda."

PART ONE

The Call of the Daemon

I think that's the purpose of a mythology that we can live by. We have to find the one that we are in fact living by and know what it is so that we can direct our craft with competence.
— Joseph Campbell

A creative person has little power over his own life. He is not free. He is captive and driven by his daimon.
— Carl Jung

1

The Hidden River of Your Writing

W E BEGIN with a chapter of multiple metaphors and perspectives. I present several ways of framing, picturing, and
understanding creativity, like a series of shifting lenses, each one
tinted a different shade and therefore highlighting, revealing, and
calling out a different aspect of the subject. This is to give us a
running start.

It also establishes an approach that I will return to throughout
the book.

Navigating the Dreamscape

This is the ultimate secret of creativity: Your whole life is a story that
you are telling. This thing you call "my life" is a dream narrative.
You are both its author and its main character. As Nietzsche noted,
"We are all greater artists than we realize." Your challenge and
calling, as both a writer and a person, is to wake up and own this.

We humans are inherently creative expressions of the intelligence that gives rise to the entire cosmos. So consciously expressing
this creative force in the form of writing, ideas, and projects
that flow through you is simply an extension of your own basic

essence. Carl Sagan famously asserted that "we are star stuff." Alan Watts frequently reiterated that the energy that moves the galaxies and causes the trees and grass to grow is what moves you, too. This includes not just our bodies but our minds, our subjective lives. In your very being, you are literally nothing but a creative expression. As the Zen koan says, "Who is the master who makes the grass green?" Answer: You are.

A helpful metaphor: Each new writing project is like a maze that shapes itself as you go. You explore, learning its logic, seeking the exit. Not incidentally (or even coincidentally), this is also how your life works. What you write is a microcosm of your soul. The labyrinth of your self is the labyrinth of your work. In both writing and living, you are simultaneously creating the maze and seeking its exit.

Another useful metaphor: Creativity is a hidden river running through your life. It created you, the dream character living out this narrative of a self in a world. It also uniquely gifts you for making things within the dream: books, ideas, more. Creativity is your origin, purpose, and destiny.

We will return to this point, this idea, this lens — the notion that creativity is simultaneously something that enables you to tell a story and something that tells the story of you — in Chapter Fourteen.

The Inner Synergy

Most people are familiar with the ancient Greek idea of the muse, the spirit or spirits that are the source of creative inspiration. The different but not unrelated Greek idea of the *daimon*, the divinely assigned and accompanying spirit that represents each person's unique character and calling, also resonates with this. These two combine to produce a practical working model for how writers can understand and approach their creativity.

Your daimon or daemon provides the fire, the enthusiasm. Your muse provides the images and ideas. Together, they make up the darkly beating heart of your creative calling: your *daemon muse*. In other words, you aren't in this alone. You have an inner partner, an inner genius. It is your creative and existential guide, your whole life GPS.

One of the most powerful actions you can take to develop a rich creative life is actually a non-action: Give up conscious control over the ultimate shape, nature, and direction of your work. Hand over the responsibility for those things to your deep self. Hand it over to the mysterious — but utterly present and vividly real — force that is your own deepest identity, the aware presence that is who you are right now, the source out of which this appearance of you as a separate individual has emerged. Recognize that your role as this seemingly separate identity is simply to midwife and refine the material that wants to be written.

It doesn't matter what you believe about the daemon muse literally or factually. To approach creative work with the mindset that you — the conscious you, ego you — really are partnered with a separate intelligence, regardless of whether you want to believe it's ultimately your unconscious mind or that it has some kind of objective reality, is the most beneficial and productive thing you can do. This approach extends beyond writing and artistic creativity as such. It's about divining your whole life direction by aligning conscious intent with unconscious will.

A Separate Intelligence

Picture creativity as something coming through you — not something you own, not yours for personal credit or blame, but a force that you serve, a separate intelligence within you. Take the view that you are the scribe, and you are the editor, but you are not the source. Whether metaphor or "really real," this works. And it better serves you, your writing, and the world.

Some people demur on this point. They place more value on what they consider to be more practical factors. They say skill, discipline, and knowledge are more vital. But those things are empty shells without inspiration. They are means, not ends.

Work without inspiration is dry and dead. But it is also true that inspiration without work is mute and meaningless. The discipline of collaborating with your daemon muse will successfully navigate you straight through the gauntlet of this creative Scylla and Charybdis.

When you learn how to approach creativity as if it's a separate force in your psyche, an autonomous intelligence, your inner genius or silent partner, you unlock the core purpose of your life, the reason why you were born. We will look at this in detail in the chapters that follow.

The Fusion of Will and Destiny

And yet, having said all the above, there is another essential point that you must not miss: Don't be a mere puppet for your daemon. When you take conscious action to reach where you want to be in life, it is critically important to remain self-aware about the very source of your wanting. Question your motivation. Realize that you are in the grip of forces that move you for reasons you can only dimly discern with your conscious, rational mind. Sometimes these inner forces are volcanic. They don't necessarily care about your individual well-being.

This raises an issue that deserves early mention in a book like this one, a book that talks about autonomous-feeling forces in the personal psyche: It's possible, and not only that, but useful, and even more, necessary for sanity and safety, to view the manifestations of the daemon as falling along a kind of spectrum. In the following three chapters, you'll see me talking about this force or figure in a variety of ways, ranging from constructive muse to destructive monster. This tension is built into the nature of the daemon itself, as recognized for more than two millennia by those who have engaged with it, reflected on it, and talked and written about it. See, for example, the ancient Greek writings about the ambiguity and duality of the *daimon* (later Latinized as *daemon*) and its incorporation into the Christian scriptures, where it is often the Greek word used in places where English translations render it as "unclean spirit" — the kind involved in cases of demonic possession — even as it also retained, in other cultural contexts down through the centuries, its different meanings associated with divine guidance, personal character, and creative destiny. You can read more about this, if you want, in my *A Course in Demonic Creativity* and my essay on the iconic figures of the Angel and the Demon in *What the Daemon Said*. For now, just understand that the different framings of the daemon that we will examine here, from the divine to the demonic, do not indicate contradiction but complementarity. Understand the daemon as a single, powerful inner force whose expression, whether constructive or destructive, is determined by the individual's degree of conscious integration and collaboration with it.

Coming into alignment with the desiring intelligence that lies behind your personal desires and motivations is the master key. Embrace it. Make friends with it. Learn to work intelligently with it. Without this inner collaboration, without a way to bring unconscious forces into harmony with your conscious mind, you are effectively a robot acting out programming that may as well be coming from someone else.

But when you do cultivate this inner alignment, your whole life becomes a sustained wave of harmonious flow, the fusion of your individual will with your given destiny, such that you can no longer distinguish, nor do you even care to distinguish, where the one ends and the other begins.

Your Unique Creative Purpose

Sometimes clichés are not trite and useless but filled with vital meaning. Here is one: Write what only you can write. Say what only you can say.

You have the one quality that nobody can ever counterfeit: You are yourself. No one else can say that. No one else now sees, or has ever seen, or will ever see the world from your unique point of view. This is the very point of the manifestation, the purpose of the dream of separation, you-plus-world, that is now unfolding.

If you write from the white-hot center of what purely fascinates you, if you write simply and directly as yourself, then originality in your writing just happens. Because you are by definition unique, your honest writing will automatically carry this same quality of uniqueness. Get in touch and in tune with your daemon muse, with the singular creative impulse that is embedded in and evinced by your life. Write from that deep creative center, from the white-hot core of the absolutely idiosyncratic vision and mission that came into the world with you, and that is uniquely yours, and that will never be fulfilled throughout all the eons — a loss to us all, the ultimate existential failure for you — unless you yourself fulfill it.

A Portable Monastery of the Muse

If you are a natural introvert whose creative impulse thrives in and on solitude, and who has felt the same impulse smothered many times by the call and clamor of the outside world, then learn this lesson: You don't need external solitude to hear the voice of your muse. You can find it right in the middle of a crowd. You can learn to carry your creative silence and solitude with you: a portable inner monastery of the muse. We will return to the monastery and monk metaphor at the end of the book.

As a writer you have to return daily to ground zero, to the quiet place inside, where the words appear. Take a minute to call your muse. Freewrite or meditate. Pause thirty seconds to ground yourself. Feel the body. Breathe. There are many easy ways to refocus and center yourself.

The lost art of making yourself unreachable, of knowing how to disappear so you can hear your muse, and not just knowing how, but having the will to do it in a society of perpetual clamor and connection — this will be the superpower of the most influential writers and creators.

Embrace solitude as a writer, even loneliness. Hear your daimon muse above the noise of the crowd. And sometimes, yes, this may require external solitude. Social media, literary conferences, writer's groups — these are all fine. Until they're not. Ernest Hemingway nailed it in his Nobel Prize acceptance speech:

> Writing, at its best, is a lonely life. Organizations for writers palliate the writer's loneliness but I doubt if they improve his writing. He grows in public stature as he sheds his loneliness and often his work deteriorates. For he does his work alone and if he is a good enough writer he must face eternity, or the lack of it, each day.

Writing and Waking Up

Creatively, you are faced with "otherness" in two directions, outward and inward. Outwardly, you are confronted by the world of people and objects, your environment. Inwardly, you are confronted from behind by your daemon muse or unconscious mind, like a separate intelligence behind your very self. And in the middle: "you." Writing is an act of joining these two, of allowing the fulcrum point of you — your rational mind, your conscious ego — to bring forth what your daemon wants to say in a form that resonates with the world. As such, writing is a means of transcending otherness by realizing your purpose. It's ultimately a healing act, something that repairs the perceived rupture in Being that creates the experience of a world at infinite odds with itself.

The primary locus of this rupture is in that very sense of separation and autonomy that you call "me." The drama of your daemon behind you and the world before you and outside you is just a shadow show, a dream of pleasure and suffering. You can write your way to waking up from it.

If you ask, "Waking up to what?" the answer is that you wake up to yourself as the dreamer, the open field of aware presence in which all experiences arise. Not any thought, emotion, image, or other experience, but what lies beyond them all and witnesses them all. This is not remote, not some distant, hopeful vision of what could or might be someday. It's what we are right now. What you discover when you turn away from literally everything that can be an object of experience, whether "inner" or "outer," is your real self as the nothing that is the precondition for anything to appear at all. Not another dream, but waking up from all dreams to remember yourself as the dreamer. If it's an experience of any kind, on any level, whether sense perception, thought, emotion, mood, sensation, mental image, or anything else, it is something perceived and not the perceiver. No object of experience is the experiencer.

That said, you can easily take the dream metaphor a bit too far. Other language can be used in talking about this. But the metaphor of the dream and the dreamer is one of the most directly applicable. When it comes to self-realization, you do not wake up to another world or set of experiences in the same way that you do when you awaken from a conventional nocturnal dream and return to the world of waking experience. Rather, you remember your identity as pure being, absolute awareness, which simply is what it is. It has no qualities, attributes, or actions, at least not as those words are conventionally defined. It seems like literally nothing to the rational mind because it cannot become an object of thought or perception. It seems like a pure absence from that perspective. But actually, right now, you and I both are that very nothing. So it's not just pure nothingness, a void in itself. It is simply awake is-ness.

And it speaks and writes through you.

2

The Daemon of Pen and Page

The Coherence of Your Self

In the late autumn of 2023, I found myself taking stock of my writing that year. And I noticed that, in a development I never would have predicted before it actually unfolded, my interaction with social media had become a source of significant authorial energy and productivity. Habitually an intermittent writer, I found that I had written a great deal that year, and that much of it had been specifically produced for sharing through a medium that I, like many people, have tended to criticize and use with more than a dash of irony.

This phenomenon was related to the fact that, beginning in the spring of that year, I adopted a fresh approach to social media in which I deliberately set out to ride the Thoreauvian railroad instead of letting it ride me. I sought out information, advice, and guidance on how to write for best effect in a short-form social media environment, with "best" judged by the metric of reader response and connection, that is, overall success or failure in communicating messages in such a way that people would actually see them and read them. This resulted not only in a noticeable increase in positive interactions with a growing crowd of readers but also in a new charge of energy infusing itself into my ongoing exploration of the intersection between the daemon muse model of writing and creativity and the theme of nondual self-realization.

This energizing effect was quite unexpected. In the course of five months, I wrote and shared thousands of words through a medium that has generally favored pithy, short-form statements stripped of rhetorical subtlety and stylistic flourishes. And somehow this shift to a new register that felt so different from my usual mode of writing unlocked a well of motivation. I found myself returning to my computer keyboard day after day as I sought to state the truth as it appeared to me in that moment. The words began to accumulate. Momentum began to build. As the weeks and months passed, I was genuinely surprised at the volume and variety of what wanted to express itself.

And then, of course, as the autumn season advanced and the shadows of its final twilight lengthened, that energy curve reached its peak and began its descent. This was predictable. For years my creative impulse has tracked the seasonal cycle. The fall and winter months usually represent a time of hibernation and incubation for my creative activity. So naturally, as that year's seasonal shift toward retreat and reflection took place, I turned to contemplating the recent spring/summer surge to see what it added up to.

What I found was right in line with something William Stafford said in an essential essay on writing that I have returned to many times in my life: "I know that back of my activity there will be the coherence of my self, and that indulgence of my impulses will bring recurrent patterns and meanings again."[1] The scattered, separate statements and reflections that I had shared on social media that year added up to several quasi-essays, appearing in fragments, written incrementally in what felt like random order over an extended span of time, and falling later into discernible groups with spontaneously logical orderings that displayed a progression of thought and theme. This happened concomitantly with the writing of the more conventionally produced essays that I thought of as such when I was publishing them in my online newsletter, *The Living Dark*. As with those, some of that other material now appears in this book.

I tell you this, including the story behind it, on the chance that it might be as valuable to you in your own creative life as it would have been to me if someone had said it years ago, early in my career, when I was mired in the unnecessary notion of a rational and linear progression of ideas and their articulation whenever I faced a blank page. Trust in the coherence of your self. Indulge your impulses. See what patterns and meanings emerge.

Importantly, do this not only when you write, but when you read, when your mind and sensibility are taking in someone else's words and seeking to assimilate them. Seek to understand what is being said, but don't ignore your own reactions to it as well, all the thoughts and feelings arising naturally within the inner space of *you* as you interact with the textually transmitted inner space of another person.

What You Seek

What are you about, really and principally, as a writer? And not only that, but what are you really and principally about as a reader?

These paired questions have become more important to me over the years. And they should be important to you, too, because the two roles are not separate. Your core orientation in each role, that of writer and that of reader, has significant implications both for your relationship to the books and writers you cherish and for your relationship to the things you write and the people who read them.

For me, figuring this out over many years has been a slow discipline of self-understanding. It has become clear over time that my authorial role, first taking form in the horror stories that I wrote, and then in my writings on creativity and spiritual awakening, has been to articulate and reinforce what my readers already, on some deep level, know. To restate the primal intuitions about writing, art, self, society, and reality that people already feel. Accompanied, yes, by a modicum of practical advice when it comes to the latter type of writing (on creativity and spirituality). But that is not my principal métier. The role I am called to take in this writer-reader relationship is a more pointedly inspirational one, an approach more of articulating and confirming than of providing concrete, practical instruction. A role of inciting and communicating a warm-electric glow of affirmation, of "Yes, that's how it is!" and "I'm so glad someone finally said this."

Unsurprisingly, I am acquainted with the powerful pleasure of reading such writing myself, of reading words that state what I have long been incubating as my own firsthand insights. From Lovecraft and Ligotti to Alan Watts and Eckhart Tolle, and from Ray Bradbury and Natalie Goldberg to Victoria Nelson and Shunryu Suzuki, I have always been riveted by the experience of reading or hearing the words of someone else who clearly, cogently, and sensitively states things that I already know, but that I know only tacitly: truths that I have deeply, murkily intuited within the privacy of my inner world. Encounters with these external reflections of my own most private thoughts, feelings, and understandings have been powerfully moving and magnetic in my life.

And beyond even that, becoming self-aware of this phenomenon, and letting it motivate and orient not only my reading but my writing — a shift that occurred over the past couple of decades as my understanding of nondual self-realization and the muse/daimon/daemon/inner genius deepened — has been nothing less than transformative.

What are you reaching for and aiming at in your own reading and writing? What are you aching to find, understand, achieve, accomplish, or realize? How are they both, in the end — your daimon of the pen and daimon of the page — one and the same?

Knowing what you are truly, deeply, centrally about as a reader/writer, two roles or identities that are inextricably paired, and bringing this core tone and purpose to bear on your actions in both areas in a way that simultaneously illuminates them and preserves their inherent mystery — this is a goal and an ideal devoutly to be pursued.

I encourage you to take some time to tap into your principal motivations, both when you read and when you write, by reflecting on them gently over time and letting an understanding of what you're really after on both fronts grow organically.

You are seeking something when you read. There's a general theme that underlies your motivation when you're drawn to read some particular thing, some specific book, author, essay, article, poem, blog post, or play. Can you see it? Can you state it?

You are also seeking something when you write, both as a general habit, practice, or calling, and as the act of working on a specific text on a given day. Some consistent purpose lies behind each individual piece or project. Can you intuit it? Can you taste it?

What is it? What motivates you? What are you reaching for and aiming at? What are you aching to find, understand, achieve, accomplish, or realize? And how are the two arenas where this motive emerges, the readerly and the writerly, related? What do they share? How does this common core, this mutually infusing urge and desire, shape your approach to each separately and the two together? How are they both, in the end — your daimon of the pen and daimon of the page — one and the same?

Even more deeply: What lies beyond and stands before both? And how is it that interrogating these things at this level becomes an exercise in triangulating the very source of your being?

Your Core Question

As has often been observed, we teach best what we most need to learn. You can turn this around to recognize your core question, your life's calling.

Your central concern is a tether that links you all the way back to your true purpose and deep identity. What's your key theme? What are you always trying to tell people? What message do you repeat in your words, whether written or spoken?

I'll take myself as an example: My own deepest concern is how to both fulfill and transcend the creative impulse of my life. This is evident from such things as the content of my books, the things I am always bringing up in conversation with other people, and what I have brought to my wildly careening career, which started in video and media production and then took a turn through the financial industry on the way to becoming an educator — first a high school teacher, then a college professor — and eventually a college vice president, all while cultivating a separate career as a writer.

In the intentions and emotions that I have brought to my various jobs; in the stories that I have written exploring the boundary between religion and horror; in my essays on the intersection of creativity with religion, spiritual awakening, life purpose, and the apocalyptic sense of a world that's breaking down; in my interactions with my readers, students, friends, and family; in the journal that I have kept for thirty years — in all of this, what I constantly circle back to and try to get at is how to understand what I'm doing here: why I was born, how I'm called, and why life, the universe, and everything, including my own existence, can seem both fascinating and fearsome, beautiful and weirdly uncanny.

Why am I built as I am, with these particular gifts and drives? Why am I planted among these specific people and circumstances at this point in history? Who or what is this "I" that views itself this way and poses these very questions?

Ultimately, I'm driven to discover or remember who I really am beyond the dream of this personal existence. This drive is both shown and concealed in the tantalizing sense of simultaneous longing and dread that I feel lurking behind the edge of my personal horizon. That's what I see when I zoom out and look at my writing and relationships, when I take the 30,000-foot view of what I have been saying, seeking, and teaching for years.

You can do the same with your own life and writing. What is your master theme? What do you most need to say, and therefore to learn? What knowledge does your life crave? What message does it speak? What purpose do you embody?

Beyond the Creative Impulse

When I speak of not only fulfilling but transcending the creative impulse, I'm referring to the motivation that I feel to let go of a grasping sort of identification with it, to ride it as a wave instead of feeling a sense of ownership. The creative impulse is only half the story in a total cycle of life purpose and fulfilled destiny.

Ultimately creativity, the "outgoing movement" from pure being, which creates the complementary pair of a separate subjective dream identity and the dream of an objective cosmos for it to inhabit, comes full circle and culminates in the return movement, when you let everything go and resume your seat in and as the Absolute, which resolves the difference between the subject-object poles. Each of us is a creative expression that arises from and returns to That. The paradox of feeling driven both to give form to creative ideas and just to let them go, drop it all, and rest placidly in the moment — something we all feel from time to time, and that some of us feel all the time — inheres in that underlying truth. The goal I feel drawn toward is to realize ever more clearly and fully the reality of this rest in motion, this grasping-less flow of creation as it both arises and subsides.

(For more on the desire to drop everything and rest, see Part Two of this book. For more on finding creative rest in creative motion, see Part Three.)

The Key to Your Life

Consider this metaphor: Your life is a locked door. It swung shut when you were born. The key to opening it is your longing, your inborn daimon.

This self you take yourself to be, this experience of being a subjective separate entity located in an objective world, stands between you and the happiness you long for. On the other side of this self-locked door is absolute fulfillment, the culmination of the infinite ache, the absolute longing for knowledge and beauty that you have always felt radiating from and shining through certain vistas, seasons, scenes, relationships, books, and music.

The answer to the question you can never quite articulate. The sight of the beauty that has always lurked behind the horizon. The full recollection of the maddening half-memory that has haunted your whole life with a cosmic sense of déjà vu. It's all hidden away behind the locked door of your life, of your very self.

There exists a perfectly fitted key. It is in the shape of your very longing itself. Your daimon, your calling, your deep, unique character. The door that swung shut when you were born from the Absolute as the expression of that outgoing daimonic impulse swings open along the same line. The way out is the way in.

Coming into conscious alignment with your daimon, your daemon, your genius, your muse, through realizing and doing what you were born to do, results not only in the fulfillment of your assignment in the world, but in the ultimate culmination of your whole life by the transcending of it. The locked door of your self swings back open, inward, when you follow the clue of that deepest yearning, that tantalizing implicit memory and calling. You walk backward through the door and resume your seat in infinity, even as you continue to see and exist in the world. The door between the two realms of the Absolute and the relative now stands open. What was formerly a barrier is now an opening. The self, the life, that was a locked door is now the very channel for the infinite to enter and illuminate everything. As Meister Eckhart said, the eye through which you see God is now the eye through which God sees you.

Again, just a metaphor, though perhaps not an idle one. A metaphor more real than literal truth, as all metaphors worth the label always are.

NOTES

1. William Stafford, "A Way of Writing," in *Writing the Australian Crawl* (University of Michigan Press, 1978), 18–19.

3

The Daemon in Exile:
A Cultural History

I BEGIN this chapter with a word of advice: You can skip it, if you prefer, as it is not strictly necessary. Your understanding of the book's overall flow of thought and argument will not be negatively affected if you just move on to the next chapter. However, the subject that I explore in this one adds background and context to our consideration of the muse and the daemon by looking at their current status in the collective consciousness of modern culture and society, especially in the West. The chapter briefly traces the ejection and exile of the daemon muse from what came to be considered respectable intellectual discourse in the age of science, rationality, and technology, and it suggests some truly awful consequences, both personal and civilizational, that have flowed from this unintelligent act. So, if such things interest you, please read on.

Also, please bear in mind that my perspective and approach here is forthrightly personal and idiosyncratic. Even when I adopt a tone of ostensible objectivity, and even when I talk about matters of factual history spanning the past few centuries, I am still speaking subjectively and offering my deeply personal and impressionistic take on things. This means my account freely foregrounds and magnifies some things while reducing or even ignoring many others that would validly form a part of the picture someone else might paint. I am aware that this may seem a dubious approach for talking about matters of objective history and collective import, and I tell you this in the spirit of full disclosure and forewarning, to help you receive these thoughts in the right way. But then, the approach I'm describing is not really different from the one I have adopted throughout the book. It's just that the specific subject matter here gives my subjective statements the sound of objective pronouncements. This is a mere artifact of language.

Consider what follows a kind of visionary history of the past several hundred years, viewed from a highly and specifically inflected angle. For me, this angle sheds light, and also creates shadows, in a way that truly illuminates. Maybe it will for you, too.

The Enlightenment's Shadow

The daemonic muse model of creativity holds that it is eminently reasonable and helpful to regard creativity as an independent force that emerges through you, as opposed to a quality or power that you possess or a feat that you're able to perform. Importantly, this ancient model of creativity is also a model of consciousness. It is a model of the nature and status of the self within the broader context of psychological life as a whole, human life in general, and the world at large.

This model, in various temporally and culturally specific forms, held steady for most of Western history. Then, beginning with the Renaissance and culminating in the eighteenth-century Age of

Enlightenment and nineteenth-century Age of Science — the latter of which, as we can now see in retrospect, might be more accurately termed the Age of Scientism — it underwent a drastic change. Western culture went through a period of enormous and energetic transformation in its fundamental understanding of what it means to be human. As one component of this, the idea of creativity, including its source and nature, could not help but be affected as well.

What happened was that the consolidation of the rational ego that occurred during this epoch — the "discovery," as it were, of the autonomous conscious subject — effectively booted the muse, the daimon/daemon, and the genius out of mainstream society and what came to be considered the only mode of respectable public discourse within the halls of scientific and intellectual power. The nineteenth century with its upsurge of wholesale scientific materialism pressed the point and accelerated the trend by ruthlessly squeezing out of its dominant worldview everything in human psychic life besides the cold eye of the rational mind. Human nature, so the thinking went, was now infinitely malleable, because in such a model what we are is solely and exclusively what we consciously are. This meant there was no room for muses or daemons, those pesky emblems and carriers of destiny and meaning "from beyond." Genius, for its part, was allowed to stick around, but in the greatly modified form of a quality inherent in a few extraordinary individuals — a far cry from the autonomous genius spirit and visiting presence that had formerly empowered the work of artists and thinkers.

Certainly, people like the Romantics, and Kierkegaard, and Nietzsche, and Jung, and even Freud helped to keep alive the recognition that our psyche is home to a great deal of non-rational stuff. But Freud's famous psychological model, which became so culturally dominant throughout the twentieth century and beyond, effectively tamed and denatured the non-rational by stripping it of metaphysical meaning and strapping it to a materialist scheme. Freud built his system firmly on a foundation of Victorian rationalism and scientism. This meant his framing of the non-rational region of the psyche inevitably portrayed it as the home of monstrous and rapacious forces, since that is the only way it can seem to the rational ego.

Moreover, Freud didn't stop at the psyche. He made pronouncements about society and civilization, declaring that human life exists in a permanent and tragic state of warfare between the rational forces of civilization and the irrational forces of our repressed id. Our only choice, as he saw it, and as he taught an entire generation or three to believe, was between a drab and rigid life of civilized order but fundamental unfulfillment of our primal impulses, or a reversion to a dark night of primal savagery. We can either be civilized and enjoy the benefits of safety and security that come with this, while enduring the lifelong denial of our primary desires, or we can give in and freely pursue the satisfaction of those cravings, leading to a Hobbesian "state of nature" with its accompanying war of all against all. Either choice results in misery. This is the cul-de-sac Freud reached in his own thinking and transmitted to the rest of us as our glum vision of things. At the end of the egoic road, we find a fork that leads to only two destinations: misery or horror.

How to Make a Monster

You only have to review the history of the twentieth century to see the effects of such attitudes on human life. This was the era when the Enlightenment ideal of rationally self-interested selves pursuing their respective happinesses was epically enabled by the birth of the first truly technological society. And it was marked by violence on a scale never before seen in human history.

The Great War of 1914 to 1918 was so called because it was the bloodiest and deadliest war ever fought, thanks to the effects of momentous technological innovations — tanks, airplanes, howitzers, mustard gas, radios, telephones — some of which, as in the case of new communications technologies, affected not only the battlefield but widespread patterns of human life leading up to and extending after the war. Then, a mere two decades later, a new and even bloodier global conflict broke out, thus demoting the Great War to the status of World War I.

And then, after the end of that war, it just kept going. There never was a real Pax Americana in the postwar period, because every decade saw more military conflicts, some involving the United States and others not. Even as many people were trying to stop thinking about the horrors of the Second World War — recall A. M. Rosenthal's suggestion, in his grim and moving 1958 *New York Times* essay "There Is No News from Auschwitz," that the Western public appeared to be making a concerted effort to forget all about the Nazi concentration camps barely more than a decade after they had been liberated — governments and nations set about creating more horrors that were going to be hard to ignore. A million and a half Armenians killed in Turkey. Stalin's starvation of seven million of his own people in Russia. The Rape of Nanking. Two million Cambodians slaughtered under Pol Pot's regime. Eight hundred thousand Tutsis slaughtered by Hutu militia in Rwanda. Two hundred thousand Muslims slaughtered by Serbs in Bosnia.

And these are only the numbers killed in explicitly genocidal operations; the actual number of people who died from various acts and campaigns of violence and oppression in the twentieth century reached into the tens or even hundreds of millions. Compare these numbers to those favorite Western historical touchstones of human cruelty, the Spanish Inquisition and the Crusades, which in tandem killed fewer than two million people. Then note that this disparity is not merely a function of lower absolute population numbers during those historical periods; the greater violence of the twentieth century was proportional as well as absolute.

To return to our main theme: One way of understanding the meaning of that awful century is to read it as a period when our collective non-rational aspect was deformed by violent repression and abandonment and then let loose via our deliberate ignorance to wreak havoc on a scale never before seen. The psychological principle that says you will inevitably be dominated and manipulated by inner forces when you are unaware of them holds true not just on the individual level but on the collective one. And so, in an epic return of the repressed, we transformed our muse, our guiding daimon, into a raging demon by denying its existence and significance, and then abandoning it to do whatever the hell it wanted.

Frankenstein's Warning

There is a notable literary parable about this very thing. Its title is *Frankenstein,* and its author was a very young Mary Shelley. It wasn't just the first science fiction novel, but the first full-on symbolic psychological exploration of the ominous meaning of the Western world's infatuation with ego consciousness to the detriment of the poetic and visionary powers. As an influential and convincing reading of the novel has long maintained, Victor Frankenstein, with his obsessive attempt to discover and then manipulate the secret of life's creation, clearly embodies the Promethean excesses of the heedless rational ego as it forgets its deep roots in primal sources of being that are no less human for being non-egoic. His monster is not just a machine-like automaton representing the dangers of scientific experimentation. Rather, it is an externalization, a kind of theurgic drawing down, of his own deeper nature, which inevitably becomes a murderous force that destroys everyone and everything Victor has ever loved, because Victor refuses to acknowledge his responsibility to it.

Victor is horrified at his own act of creating this being, and by the monster's hideous physical appearance. This reaction is the inevitable effect of his attempt to become nothing but a rational ego, a perfect scientist in the eighteenth- and nineteenth-century mode. The creature, his rejected visionary and poetic powers, his rejected unconscious mind or muse, seems to him the epitome of everything loathsome and hateable. And, in the manner common to this subtle and shady-seeming part of our psyches, it helplessly obliges this perception by accepting this projection and becoming the monster it is seen to be.

That mad scientist is each of us when we fail to take into account the reality, autonomy, integrity, and needs of our deep muse-self, not only in creative artistic work, but in life as a whole, and not only in our individual lives, but in the life of human societies and all humankind. That loathsome, murderous, and deeply pitiable monster is our muse, our daemon, our genius become overtly demonic because we have severed it from our attentions and affections and thereby let it become a force that can affect us as an afflicting "other," outside our ability to control or commune with it. There is a reason why the idea of "making a Frankenstein's monster" has become idiomatically entrenched in our collective consciousness.[1]

Compound this problem several billion times over in the communal life of the people inhabiting our planet, and you have a picture of the world we have built by denying our daemon. We are Victor Frankenstein, and our dark side only appears as such and continues to cause such trouble because we have made it that way.

Monsters and Angels

What is the ultimate and final benefit of embracing your genius, meeting your muse, aligning with your daemon? It is simply that you heal this epic rift by owning up to what is really true of your personal experience, what is really true in a deeply human sense. You account for a missing part of yourself that, if you are at all a typical member of the culture in which and to which I am speaking, you have not been given an adequate set of concepts and attitudes for recognizing. The polar opposite of the demon-haunted life we have been living together for over a century can be seen in the case of those writers and artists who have learned to commune and collaborate with the nightside of their psyche, and whose lives have been blessed because of it.

One of my favorite examples of such a person is Ray Bradbury, whose work and person have played an outsized inspirational role in my life (an experience that I know is hardly unique to me). Bradbury's wisdom and insight on the subject of writing and creativity are well known, and here I want to call attention to three different statements that he made on three separate occasions, several years apart. When considered together, these statements express the solution to our problem and provide a blueprint for integrated living.

In 2004, when he was 84 years old and nearing the end of a legendary career as one of the most prolific, important, and beloved writers of fantasy, horror, and science fiction, Bradbury told an interviewer for Fox News, "All of my writing is God-given. I don't write my stories — they write themselves. So out of my imagination, I create these wonderful things, and I look at them and say, My God, did I write that?" The interviewer, seeking clarity, asked, "So they all just came to you? You can't explain it?" And Bradbury answered: "Everything comes to me. Everything is my demon muse. I have a muse which whispers in my ear and says, 'Do this, do that,' but it's my demon who provokes me."[2]

Some unspecified time before that (but not very long), Bradbury said something to his biographer, Sam Weller, that further rounded out his perspective on an entire way of life. Weller asked, "Do you ever read your old books and short stories once they've been published?"

Bradbury replied, "Every so often, late at night, I come downstairs, open one of my books, read a paragraph and say, 'My God.'

I sit there and cry because I haven't done any of this. It's a God-given thing, and I'm grateful, so grateful." He went on to assert that this sense of not having written the works bearing his name, but of instead having simply received them, imparted a divinely mythic character to his whole career: "The best description of my career as a writer is, 'At play in the fields of the Lord.' It's been wonderful fun, and I'll be damned where any of it came from."[3]

Finally, in December 2002, at the age of 82, Bradbury ended the introduction to *Bradbury Stories*, a collection of his most famous and beloved tales, by saying the following: "My eyes fill with tears as I review the table of contents of this volume — all my dear, dear friends — the monsters and angels of my imagination."[4]

There it is. The complete profile. The recipe for living: Everything is my demon muse. My muse whispers what to do while my demon provokes me. It's God-given. I have been at play in the fields of the Lord with my dear friends, the monsters and angels of my imagination.

To drive home the point, contrast Ray Bradbury, whose inner monsters and angels were his dear friends, with Victor Franken-stein, for whom the same forces were a demonic affliction that de-stroyed everyone and everything he loved. Or compare Bradbury with Western civilization, which has torn itself and the world apart by exiling its monsters, its angels, its collective daemon muse, to the outer darkness of oblivion — where, as we have said, such things do not disappear but instead transform into extra-cosmic monsters that inevitably return to puncture the rim of our universe and inundate us with a primordial flood of uncontrollable — because unembraced and unidentified with — violence and chaos of the non-rational.

Bradbury definitely grasped the point in his own life, and he used it as his guiding star, embracing his daemon muse and channeling it into a body of work that fulfilled his purpose and enriched us all. The question that presents itself to each of us, simply by virtue of the fact that we have been born as these strange and curious beings with a divided inner life that contains all these potentialities, is whether we can do this, too. Can we intuit our way to an inner relationship of harmony with our daemon, thus enabling the outpicturing of a self/world pairing that isn't monstrous, but that instead represents a life at play in the divine fields with our beloved monsters and angels?

Consider it carefully. Your whole world is waiting for your answer.

NOTES

1. For an in-depth reading of Mary Shelley's novel along the lines that I am laying out here, see my essay "Those Sorrows Which Are Sent to Wean Us from the Earth: The Failed Quest for Enlightenment in Mary Shelley's *Frankenstein*," in my *What the Daemon Said.*

2. Catherine Donaldson-Evans, "An Interview With Sci-Fi Legend Ray Bradbury," *Fox News*, November 23, 2004, *https://www.foxnews.com/story/an-interview-with-sci-fi-legend-ray-bradbury.*

3. Sam Weller, *Listen to the Echoes: The Ray Bradbury Interviews* (Stop Smiling Books, 2010), 223.

4. Ray Bradbury, *Bradbury Stories: 100 of His Most Celebrated Tales* (William Morrow, 2005), xvii.

4

Meet Your Inner Genius

PRACTICALLY speaking, the most basic statement of truth about writing and creativity in relation to the inner genius is this: You are not ultimately responsible for it. You are responsible for befriending your creativity. You are responsible for practicing the craft side of it so that you can forge yourself into a channel, an instrument, a conduit for its clear and truthful expression. You are responsible for actively waiting on it to court its presence and ensure you're ready when it chooses to alight. As Picasso famously said, "Inspiration exists, but it has to find you working."

But as for generating it, or controlling it, or determining its nature, content, or deep direction — these are beyond you. Their responsibility belongs to the creative spirit itself. Your job as a writer is not to "be creative" but to shepherd your unique creative spirit into the world through a rich discipline of inner collaboration. In such work, the operative principle is: Give your daemon its due.

A Sense of Inner Otherness
Of course, to say such things and use such language is to raise many questions. It may all sound interesting to some people,

especially creatively oriented types like you and me, but it also begs the question of whether we are talking about something real or imaginary. Is the daemon a metaphor, or are we talking about a literal reality?

The question of creativity's ultimate source is an old one. And a fascinating one. Historically, attempts to answer it have often led into the realms of the spiritual, the esoteric, and the occult, where muses, daimons, daemons, and genii hover all around us in imaginal hyperspace, whispering ideas and inspiration into the ears of poets, artists, historians, philosophers, and madmen.

More recently, in the past couple of centuries, creativity has become a popular topic in the realms of psychology and neurology. The id, the collective unconscious, the right cerebral hemisphere, the temporal lobe, the cerebellum, the pineal gland, and various other psychological and neurobiological structures and interrelationships have been named and championed as the real "muse." The shift has been away from belief in an objectively real spiritual source to the belief that inspiration is a purely subjective experience with biological and psychological causes. Which direction a person tends to lean — toward a forthrightly spiritual(ish) interpretation or a reductive scientific/materialist one — depends on their philosophical sensibility and cast of mind.

Some intrepid souls with fertile imaginations and the gift or curse of divergent thinking, plus a constitutional tendency to embrace a Robert Anton Wilsonian attitude of "maybe logic," have embraced both views.[1] Such people — and I'm one of them — say creativity is equally well explained on the one hand by biology + psychology + culture, and on the other hand as the workings of a real daemon muse or inspiring spirit. Such people (and I'm still one of them) also tend to view the rest of life and the universe at large through the same imaginally tinted pair of philosophical eyeglasses.

Having said all that, let me say it all again differently, and maybe better: I hold the whole matter of the daemon muse or inner genius in a permanent liminal hyperspace, and I suggest you join me in this. Our epistemic position makes it flatly impossible for us to know the literal truth or untruth of the daemon muse hypothesis. Wilson's famous stance of "model agnosticism" — the skeptical refusal to select or adopt any one worldview or philosophical model as privileged or absolutely true—pointedly applies to this matter. (For his winsomely riveting presentation of this position, see the opening pages of his book *Cosmic Trigger*.)

What we can know for sure is that there is incontrovertibly the feeling of another intelligence accompanying our ego self and rational mind "from behind," within our own subjectivity. In other words, the sense of it, at least, is definitely real and not in question. Any interpretations that we apply to this sense, however, whether in terms of the unconscious, the daemon, or anything else, are only that: interpretations. The datum of the experience itself remains primary.

Not tangentially, this same impossibility of final certitude applies to any and all totalizing interpretations that we place on ourselves, the world, and reality as a whole. As a matter of self-evident truth, we can never stand apart from our subjectivity, our first-personhood, to comment with objective finality on any of this.

Or rather, and to say the same thing differently and more deeply:

The only final stance is one of true objectivity, from which position the entirety of the cosmic drama, including both its subjective and objective realms, components, or aspects, is a collective wave pulse of mere appearances. Our own creativity, consisting of the dream of being a separate self that exists in perpetual relationship with a personal creative daemon, occurs within and as a component of that.

Meeting Your Daemon

Encountering your daemon and verifying its reality and presence is like the fish becoming aware of water. It's a moment of self-awareness in which you notice something that has always been present, but that was so all-pervasive in your total experience that you were unable to see it.

On a more ominous note, instead of asking how you can encounter it and verify its reality, you could just as well ask how you can get away from it. To which the answer — which elucidates the answer to the flipside question as well — is that you can't.

There are multiple ways to divine your daemon that are readily available to you, right at this moment. They aren't as esoteric as the name "daemon" and the connotations sometimes attached to it might lead you to think. For example, you can look to:

- your innate interests
- your dreams
- the things you helplessly love
- the things you helplessly hate
- the external themes of relationship and circumstance that seem to constellate as spontaneously repeated patterns over your lifetime

Any or all of these can help to clarify both the presence and the particular nature of your daemon, especially when you reframe them as questions that you're asking about someone else in an attempt to understand their personality. For example, on the question of your interests, consider this progression of thought:

- What am I really and genuinely interested in? What subjects, people, environments, thoughts, conversations, books, movies, ideas, activities, and pursuits do I find intrinsically, unself-consciously fascinating? Which ones have been with me since childhood?

- Where do these interests and inclinations come from? Why am I interested in these things and not others? Why do some things leave me cold while others light me up with instant warmth and passion? Even if I can relate my attractions to specific life events and experiences, why did I react that way when other people would have reacted — and have reacted, and did react — differently? What made the difference? What still makes it today?

- If my interests and reactions are in some irreducible measure involuntary, spontaneous, outside my conscious control, then who or what is in charge of them?

You can follow the same process of inquiry for your dreams, loves, hates, and external life configurations. Take stock of them. Identify them. Then ask what they inversely point back toward. What lies behind or before them as their deep source? The point where they converge is your daemon.

You can also do exercises like focused freewriting, especially right after you wake up in the morning, when your egoic mind is relatively subdued and your unconscious is still ascendant. Do a mind dump onto two or three pages. Practice this for a week or a month. Then reread what you've written, poring over the text in search of discernible patterns and themes. If you'd like more detailed guidance or advice on this, Julia Cameron is the most prominent English-language source of advice on freewriting for creative self-discovery, in her now classic practice of morning pages, as introduced and explained in her book *The Artist's Way*.

Other books with useful guidance on freewriting and other practices that can introduce you to your daemon muse include Dorothea Brande's 1934 classic *Becoming a Writer*, containing page after page of practical guidance for befriending your unconscious self in a partnership of mutually supportive flow; Natalie Goldberg's *Writing Down the Bones*; Brenda Ueland's *If You Want to Write*; and David Morrell's *The Successful Novelist*, with a fine chapter on discovering your native theme and direction as a writer. Ray Bradbury's *Zen in the Art of Writing* — one of the best books on the subject — brims with excellent advice on establishing a relationship of flow and fire with your unconscious genius. Especially see Bradbury's famous exercise on making lists of power nouns that name the things you are naturally impelled to write about from your life experiences and deep fascinations. His own list includes items like The Skeleton, The Ravine, The Carnival, The Lake, The Ferris Wheel, and The Dwarf — all things that readers of his work will immediately recognize as touchstone themes in his stories and novels.

You can also undertake meditative practices that enable you to watch the play of your verbal and visual minds without getting lost in them, so that you can reflect on them and recognize what they are telling you about the character of your inner collaborator. You can do this through, for example, Zen-like sitting meditation, which is my personal favorite, or through visualization practices like Jungian active imagination, which I have also benefited from.

In all such exercises, you are tuning in to the fact that you, meaning ego-you, the conscious self that says "I," are always accompanied on the subjective side of the subject-object barrier — behind your eyes, you might say — by an energetic presence that is the source of your spontaneous thoughts, desires, fears, aversions, emotional fluctuations, and general life orientation and set of predilections. It gives rise to your ideas. It forms the core of your unchosen character and personal disposition. It has been the barometer and compass of your inner world and your responses to the outer world since childhood. This is what we mean when we talk about the writer's daemon.

Strangely, this same internal presence also frequently and uncannily crosses over to the "other side" and presents itself in the events and arrangements of your external world, if you pay sufficiently close attention to notice it. As inside, so outside. As above, so below.

This last point expands the matter into the realms of esoteric and occult practices that form a long and venerable tradition, such as the "great work" of connecting with one's Guardian Angel as practiced in ceremonial magical/magickal traditions, including Thelema and the Hermetic Order of the Golden Dawn. Though I have never practiced any of these myself, I have studied them as an intellectual matter with considerable interest over the years, and I can attest that even a mere conceptual understanding of them can be significantly clarifying.

Separating Spiritual Signal From Psychological Noise

In getting to know your daemon, an immediate challenge presents itself: How can you be sure of which voice you're hearing when you direct your attention inward? We all live with a kind of inner cacophony most of the time, unless and until we have learned to silence it or dissociate ourselves from it. It can be hard to identify your daemon muse amid the chatter. Recall what I said above about learning to meditate. The spiritual teacher Bob Fergeson has advanced the term "the listening attention" to refer to a state of awareness that we can cultivate in which we watch the mind's contents, and also objective or external events, without craving them, resisting them, or getting lost in them, and in which we learn to hear the voice of our intuition. His book of that title, *The Listening Attention*, might be helpful to you.

One thing you might try — and this is something that has helped me — is what we might call the Zen trick of tuning in to sensory experience. You can do it right now: Your mind is filled at the moment with the flow of these very words. Look away from the page or screen, or close your eyes, and give a moment's attention to what's going on in your hearing. Or tune in to the physical sensations of your body, or another sense. Take note of the wordless reality of whatever is happening. This can really quiet you down, introducing a dose of significant stillness into your inner space, even if you do it for only a few seconds. Consider practicing this occasionally throughout the day, when you're walking, or riding, or driving, or eating, or buying, or interacting with other people. Most of us are so locked into our mental world for most of our waking hours that we hardly notice the other levels and layers of reality that are unfolding easily, naturally, and also richly in our experience but outside our conscious awareness. Making time to focus on them is a great way to clear out some inner space, and from there to be better able to distinguish the voice of something within us that is beyond us.

You may also need to key some of this to your own unique personality. This might require acts of discipline to protect your inner space from needless distraction. To take myself as an example, I have an extremely musical mind. I had nine years of classical piano lessons in my youth, and I have played the piano avidly since I was eight years old. My mind and sensibility respond powerfully to music, including what I hear from the outside. One aspect or side effect is that I am highly susceptible to musical earworms. I frequently enjoy listening to recorded music, but I also often find that it leaves an after-echo in my mind.

For instance, if a song grabs me when I listen to it while driving home from work, I may find it stuck in my head all evening. I may even keep hearing it, or snatches of it, in my inner mind for three or four days. Sometimes I don't even have to hear it from the outside; sometimes music — including utterly new music, original inner compositions — just comes to me spontaneously from within. This can become exhausting. Moments of pure inner silence seem precious by comparison. So I have found that I need to limit my musical consumption deliberately. Sometimes the mere act of sitting, working, or driving in silence instead of indulging in a beloved song or playlist — and using this time to tune in to the wavelength of sensory experience as described above — results in an upwelling of creative motivation, insights, and energy. You might be able to find similar little acts of austerity in your own life to loosen the habits that you unwittingly allow to limit you, thus opening up space for your daemon muse to make itself known.

Your Inner Creative Collaborator

It is helpful to consider what this kind of inner collaboration looks like in actual practice. Rudyard Kipling famously said that when you are in the grip of your daemon, your task as a writer is to "drift, wait, obey." If you're like me, you find that specific descriptions of writers in the very act of following Kipling's advice — writers who are tuned in to their creativity and following its spontaneous flow — are fascinating, clarifying, and deeply reassuring.

Just such a thing is provided by the Italian novelist and poet Andrea Bajani in a 2022 essay.[2] What's more, Bajani wraps it in a memorable metaphor that is, for me at least, one of the more valuable and winsome ways of describing the writing process that I have ever come across.

Bajani describes in intimate detail his daily habit, which he says he has practiced for many years, of walking seven minutes across town, away from his home, to do his writing in a small, solitary office. Once there, he says his work takes the form of fishing in an inner void. He sits there "on the bank of this void, staring into it, hoping for a ripple, waiting for the line to grow taut, for a word to take the bait." When something does strike at last, he says that if he is lucky enough to find a sentence or even a whole story, "then we have a meal." However, sometimes as he seeks to reel the thing in "from the nothing where it swam," what he finds is just an empty hook. When this happens, he simply "toss[es] everything back into the void" and continues waiting until nightfall, which marks the end of his workday. At that point, "I close my laptop, not a single word added, and leave for home."

I find this neat. More than that, I find it lovely. The image of writing as fishing in an inner void, casting a line into a psychic ocean, resonates powerfully.

It also links up in interesting ways with the idea of inner collaboration with the daemon muse. Am I stretching things, making an unwarranted or arbitrary leap, if I frame both Bajani's daily walk and his act of "fishing in the void" as being motivated by and performed in the service of his daemon? And if I see his daemon reflected at all points in his process?

As I see it, Bajani has successfully divined his daemon's preferred mode and external environment for working: alone, isolated from his home and wife, situated a short but definite remove from his domestic environment. His daemon accompanies him as he makes his daily seven-minute pilgrimage to his private writing monastery, brooding with him and anticipating the creative encounter that will take place there. It watches over his shoulder and looks out through his eyes with him as he casts a line into that void. It sits with him at his keyboard, waiting.

Moreover, it is the very thing he is waiting on. As he waits for a strike on the line, for some tangible form to coalesce from the inner deep and take the bait, it's as if he is fishing for his own daemon in the guise of Proteus, the ancient Greek sea god who perpetually metamorphosed into an infinitude of different shapes.

In other words, Bajani's daemon is searching for itself through him. It is the motivating force behind his creative ritual, even as it is also the elusive presence swimming in those psychic depths, the idea that strikes on the other end of the line and then reveals itself in some specific form when reeled in by his typing. It is also what sometimes slips the hook and leaves him with nothing.

Nothing, that is, except itself, still perched there with him in that silent, solitary office, urging him to complete the ritual, to put in his time, and then to do it all again the next day.

Becoming a Prepared Instrument

When considering, reflecting on, and moving to implement all of this in your own creative life and work, always remember that learning to recognize, trust, and collaborate with your daemon muse does not "let you off the hook." It may be tempting to think you can just rely on your feelings, trust your daemon, and go about your other business while your creative work takes care of itself. You may be tempted to devalue such things as practice, studying craft, and developing technical skills. To give in to this temptation would be a grave mistake.

Deliberate practice is absolutely part of what we're talking about here. All the activities that might fall under this label are fruitful, helpful, and also necessary to the extent that an individual finds them to be so. If it happens in a person's experience that simply reading, writing, and editing with an eye and ear trained on the daemon muse successfully serves to shape and develop their organism and individuality into the prepared instrument that it needs to be, then wonderful. But a more deliberate engagement with practice and training is likely to be helpful or necessary for most of us at some point.

The principle of becoming a prepared instrument is the key. Remember, this is an inner collaboration, and one of the primary parts of this relationship on our end is to train, develop, and refine ourselves, our technical skills, our sensibility, and whatever else needs to be perfected in this way, so that we're actually able to give voice and embodiment to the inspiration when it arrives.

I sometimes think of it in connection with the parallel principle of being fluent in a language — or not. Other than in those rare cases of spirit possession or other scenarios where people spontaneously begin to speak a language they hadn't previously known — which does occur — it's simply the case that fluency in any language is acquired along the conventional lines of learning it through deliberate study and/or living immersion. This being the case, it's illuminating to consider what might happen if a muse or daemon began to whisper inspiration into the inner mind of an English-only speaker for a book or poem that was meant to emerge in Italian, or Japanese, or some other language the person didn't have access to. Leaving aside the fact that in this imaginary case a definite portion of blame might be laid on an inept muse, there's the fact that on the human side the inspiration would be lost, aborted, a misfire if the person didn't take deliberate steps to learn the language and thus render him/herself able to midwife the inspiration into the world.

The same principle extends to encompass such things as technical and stylistic skills for writers, musicians, artists, and everyone else — even entrepreneurs. If you're visited by a sudden, explosive, visionary idea for a new company whose mission, nature, and actions could potentially change the world, but you have absolutely no knowledge, skills, or abilities when it comes to business, then you had better get to studying up on things like business plans, market research, financial management, strategic planning, marketing, and customer service, or else the thing will be lost, or will move on to someone else until it finds the right channel. In all these cases, deliberate practice is valuable and necessary. It's not an either/or situation in which you either develop and rely on skills or trust and listen to your daemon muse. It's a complementary both/and situation in which each depends on and fulfills the other.

Haunted From Within

Even as the idea of the daemon muse and the art of inner collaboration can strike one as interesting, even fascinating, it may also carry an unsettling note. The idea of sharing your interiority with "something else" can seem disturbing. What can you do if this is the case?

The first thing to note is that a certain feeling of fear is understandable. The sense of relating to an "other" within oneself is frankly uncanny. In fact, there are distinct parallels between the idea and experience of the daemon and the signature artistic-emotional effect of the literary subgenre of weird horror. Both dive into the murky unknown and invoke feelings you can't quite describe. The daemon is a mysterious presence playing hide and seek in the psyche, just like the elusive object of fascination and fear in a story by Lovecraft, Blackwood, or Ligotti. Your demon muse haunts you with — and more, it haunts you as — an aspect of your very self, just like the numinous dread that pervades a weird horror story. To live in conscious communion with your muse or daemon is like living in a darkly enchanted universe.

Still, this very fact contains the seed of its own solution. To be afraid of your daemon is to fear an aspect of your very self. The experience of the daemon or muse is essentially dissociative. It's one part of the psyche, the ego, experiencing another part as separate or different, as an autonomous presence or intelligence with which the ego "I" interacts. Perhaps, as suggested above, some form of meditation practice, or a focused practice of journaling or morning writing — or maybe some form of integrative psychotherapy such as Jungian analysis — could advance you past fearing this aspect of your self to partnering with it, embracing it, and eventually reclaiming it and identifying with it.

On this count, Dorothea Brande's *Becoming a Writer*, already mentioned, and also Victoria Nelson's *On Writer's Block* — a personal favorite that, in my estimation, is woefully obscure (its original title was *Writer's Block and How to Use It*) — contain some of the very best advice, specifically aimed at writers, on learning to relate well to your "inner other" in a way that both harmonizes your psyche and unlocks your ability to write in flow.

The Daemon and the Demon
Another challenge or difficulty may arise, one that is related to

but distinct from the possibility of feeling fear at the sheer fact of your inner other. Isn't there a moral danger in all this? Can't the idea of pushing creativity off onto a daemon be used in destructive ways? Can't it be used to avoid or reject responsibility for your actions? If you use your creativity for illegal or immoral purposes, can you just blame your daemon and expect to get away with it?

This approach has certainly been practiced before, the self-serving strategy of excusing bad behavior by saying, "The devil made me do it." The fact that there is such a well-known saying to refer to it indicates how common it has been in human history. It is possible for me — I, the ego — to use the concept of the daimon or daemon as a scapegoat. But the real question in such cases cuts below the surface to a subtler level, where it is turned on its head: Who is using whom? What motivates someone to commit an illegal or immoral act in the first place? The source of motivation, predilection, and personal character is the daemon itself. In light of this, is it correct to say that a person might use creativity for wrongful purposes and then blame their daemon to escape culpability as an ego self? Or is it more correct to say that the daemon uses the person?

One of the native functions and tasks of the ego, perhaps *the* native task, the implanted calling, is to negotiate and coordinate, and ideally, ultimately, to harmonize, the inward/outward relationship between the unconscious daemon and the collective external world. So the very fact of being here and awake as an ego in the world carries a real measure of responsibility for making intelligent and ethical choices. However, the additional fact that, as noted, a person's overall motivation and center of gravity emanates from the daemon complicates the matter in immediate and subtle ways.

For an insightful handling of this question — the question of how to understand and respond to the real phenomenon of the "bad daimon," the inborn negative impulse that appears to shape some people's lives, so that in them and through them the daemonic manifests as demonic — I suggest reading James Hillman's *The Soul's Code*, and specifically the chapter titled "The Bad Seed," where Hillman addresses this question in the lives of notable historical figures, especially Hitler. He offers helpful thoughts on how to understand and respond to this phenomenon, including a list of qualities in a person that may indicate the presence of a negative daemon. The astute and sensitive upshot of Hillman's handling of this seems to be that evil is something we have to account for in our societal, psychological, and even metaphysical maps, so that we can maintain intelligent ways of handling it instead of being perpetually blindsided and overcome by it.

Since one of the bad-seed qualities that Hillman names is an almost fanatical attitude of unwavering certainty about oneself and one's visions and goals, to the point of being heedless of all other considerations — including the presence and welfare of other people — you can put your mind at ease about whether you are personally possessed of a bad daemon. If you were, you probably wouldn't even be asking the question.

The bottom line in all of this is that writing is not a solo job, a solitary act of creativity. It involves a profound inner partnership. The invitation is to give up control and welcome the unexpected. What you ultimately discover over a lifetime of this inner collaboration is not just your authorial voice or vision, but your whole personal destiny.

Here is a truth that I wish I had learned earlier: My life is not my own. My goals are not my own. My destiny is not my own. Whenever I have thought and acted as if I'm in complete control, meaning has vanished and things have gone awry. My one ultimately valid choice is to give up total control, to use what little control I seem to possess to consciously accept that I was born with an inbuilt character and calling, and to work toward aligning with that instead of acting as if I'm a pure free agent in the world.

Of course, in the end this flips around and transforms into the realization that I do have control. Absolute and total control, in fact. But this involves waking up to the truth that what I mean when I say "I" is so much more than this little ego with my name attached to it, which the world has programmed me to mistake for my real self.

This awakening enables me, it enables *you*, to get your self-esteem and life fulfillment from something besides yourself, from something beyond yourself, from who you are beyond the name and form that the world has taught you to label as "you." Contrary to popular mainstream life advice, it's counterproductive to believe in yourself. Your belief in being a separate self at all is the very source of your deepest problem. Wake up to who and what you really are, and disbelieve in your conventional, society-created ego persona. Be your real self. Then the mask of your persona can safely do what it was born to do.

This kind of fulfillment and this kind of positive self-regard, which extends outward into a similar positive regard and attitude of fulfillment toward other people, is truly valid and not just an ego trip, precisely because it is not of the ego.

And what's more: It is invulnerable.

NOTES

1. For more on the term "maybe logic," see the 2003 documentary film of that title, which details Wilson's claim — elaborated over several decades and dozens of talks — that absolute certitude about anything is impossible in a universe where the entanglement of the observer with the observed and the mutual influence of each upon the other rule out the possibility of a neutral platform. Hence, the need for a logic of "maybe" to supplement or replace the more common logic of dogmatic true or false. The full film is available at *https://youtu.be/A7N6TOFyrLg?si=LCtaswkTRH22V9lQ*, with a transcript available (at least when I last checked in August 2025) at *https://antilogicalism.com/2016/05/06/maybe-logic*. For the probable origin of the term "maybe logic" in Wilson's life and thought, see his essay, "The Universe Contains a Maybe," in his 1982 book *Right Where You Are Sitting Now: Further Tales of the Illuminati*. There, he recounts listening to a lecture by physicist Dr. David Finkelstein while attending a 1979 conference at California's Monterey Conference Center — which would five years later serve as the birthplace of TED Talks — titled "Transition 21: The Emerging 21st Century." Dr. Finkelstein gave a tour of the paradoxes of quantum mechanics, compared them to modern poetry, and suggested that answers or explanations to these mysteries would necessarily come from outside the realm of Aristotelian either/or logic. As Wilson recalled, Finkelstein told the audience, "In addition to a yes and a no, the universe contains a maybe" (see Robert Anton Wilson, "The Universe Contains a Maybe," in *Right Where You Are Sitting Now*, And/Or Press, 1982, 35–50).

2. See Andrea Bajani, "Love Is Space: Notes on Marriage and Creativity," translated by Elizabeth Harris, *Literary Hub*, May 2, 2022, *https://lithub.com/love-is-space-notes-on-marriage-and-creativity*.

5

To Thine Own Muse Be True

When the Daemon Speaks

I grew up in an Independent Christian Church, one of those evangelical Protestant congregations that represent the rightward-leaning doctrinal divergence of some conservative Restoration Movement churches from their liberal brethren during the early and middle parts of the twentieth century. A motto and core principle of my childhood church, which I learned directly from my father's lips, is this: "Where the scriptures speak, we speak; where the scriptures are silent, we are silent."

Anybody who senses in this saying a close analog to the muse/daemon/genius-based approach to artistic creativity is surely onto something. You simply cannot know your innate creative rhythm — whether occasional, erratic, or prolific — until you actually do the work of finding out who you are by making friends with your daemonic genius, and then by approaching your work openly and experimentally in order to discover the pace and volume at which your creativity wants to emerge. There is a wide variation among different writers and artists in how their creative daemon consents to being accessed and how their muse consents to being courted. The crucial thing is to get in touch, and then stay in touch, with your own daemon muse, so that when it speaks, you speak, and when it is silent, you remain silent.[1]

An important implication of this truth is that you do not have to be actively writing all the time. Silence and inactivity are perfectly fine. Conversely, making space for your muse to speak when it wants by committing yourself to a regular practice can be valuable. This is not a contradiction but a simple fact of the situation, which is subtle and therefore calls for subtlety and sensitivity in one's approach.

I have always found it reassuring to read about the lives and creative habits of other writers, and especially the actual words of those who have generously talked about their idiosyncratic personal working relationship to their creative spirit. Here are six examples — from writers including Flannery O'Connor, Stephen King, and Katherine Anne Porter — illustrating the absolute viability of all positions on the matter of disciplined regular work versus the free acceptance of erratic silences. The first three line up on one side of the fence, the latter on the other. Every one of them is right, since "right" is a sliding scale calibrated to the precise nexus of karmic forces that has converged upon and manifested as the specific human being who is speaking, writing, and reflecting on these things.

Magnetizing the Muse Through Disciplined Labor

FLANNERY O'CONNOR: Three hours every morning

Flannery O'Connor was a firm believer in the value of discipline in a writer's life. She famously suffered from lupus, which was both a help and a hindrance in her attempt to maintain the discipline of a strict writer's routine. On the one hand, the severe pain of the condition took away her ability to perform many daily activities, thus leaving her free to sit and write. On the other hand, this was a sword with a distinct double edge, since, as anyone suffering from a rheumatic illness can tell you, sitting for long periods with such a condition can produce as much discomfort as moving.

This makes O'Connor's now-famous recommendation that writers ought to sit for several hours and do nothing else but write all the more striking. When her friend Cecil Dawkins complained about a dry spell that she was experiencing, and said she sometimes used reading to distract herself from the tedium, O'Connor responded with this:

> It is my considered opinion that one reason you are not writing is that you are allowing yourself to read in the time set aside to write. You ought to set aside three hours every morning in which you write or do nothing else; no reading, no talking, no cooking, no nothing, but you sit there. If you write all right and if you don't all right, but you do not read; whether you start something different every day and finish nothing makes no difference; you sit there. It's the only way, I'm telling you. If inspiration comes you are there to receive it, you are not reading.[2]

As seen in editor Rosemary Magee's 1987 anthology *Conversations with Flannery O'Connor*, O'Connor returned repeatedly to this point, stating it in various contexts and ways that, taken together, leave no doubt about her position:

> "People seem to surround being-a-writer with a kind of false mystique, as if what is required to be a writer is a writer's temperament," she says. "Most of the people I know with writer's temperaments aren't doing any writing." Miss O'Connor is writing steadily three hours a day, regardless of her mood. "If I waited on inspiration, I'd still be waiting," she says.... "I can't seem to turn out more than two stories a year. I have to have a 'story' in mind — some incident or observation that excites me and in which I see fictional possibilities — before I can start a formal piece. But I do try to write at least three hours every morning, since discipline is so important.... I sit there before the typewriter three hours every day and if anything comes I am there waiting to receive it."[3]

DANI SHAPIRO: Attract the muse with hard work

Novelist and memoirist Dani Shapiro has described her experiences with inspiration and their relationship to conscious discipline in a way that resonates warmly with O'Connor's account. Shapiro says that if she had assented to the notion that she ought to wait for inspiration before she started writing, she probably would not have written any books. "Don't get me wrong," she clarifies. "Inspiration has come. It has tiptoed into my writing room when I've least expected it. It has shown up mid-sentence, mid-thought, mid-idea. But it generally doesn't precede me to the desk." She draws out the point in a direct statement of the principle:

> Inspiration comes out of doing the work: the hard labor
> of laying each brick on top of the next, one at a time, un-
> til what you've done begins to resemble a wall. Often, it
> doesn't resemble a wall, or it's come out crooked, or in
> some way less than you'd hoped, and you have to smash
> the thing up and start all over again. Inside this painstak-
> ing labor is where inspiration lies. Only when you're up
> to your eyeballs, covered in dust, hopeless and bordering
> on despair, does the muse even consider paying a visit.[4]

STEPHEN KING: Give your muse a place to live
Stephen King has famously characterized the muse as a rough-hewn
guy in the basement of the psyche who displays a somewhat surly
demeanor and demands that you do most of the work before he
will give you anything. "He's not going to come fluttering down
into your writing room and scatter creative fairy-dust all over your
typewriter or computer station," King said in his memoir *On Writing*.
The muse "lives in the ground" and is "a basement guy" whose
personality is such that you have to go down to his level, give him
a place to live, and then "do all the grunt labor... while the muse
sits and smokes cigars and admires his bowling trophies and pre-
tends to ignore you."

However, beneath this gruff and uninviting exterior, says King,
there is real magic waiting to be bestowed. All you have to do, as
stated, is work for it. You have to labor actively instead of waiting
idly, approaching writing as a practical job like laying pipe or driving a truck. It is this regularity that woos the muse and eventually

wins him over to your side. "Your job," said King, "is to make sure the muse knows where you're going to be every day from nine 'til noon or seven 'til three. If he does know, I assure you that sooner or later he'll start showing up, chomping his cigar and making his magic."[5]

O'Connor, Shapiro, and King — all three are in agreement that inspiration is not something to be passively waited for but something to be actively invited through a regular schedule of disciplined work. Personally, I find this resonates. It carries the ring of intuitive truth. It feels organically complete and satisfying, like a statement of core insight. In fact, I have often taken it as such in my own work, and have issued it as a recommendation to others.

However, there is a counter-opinion, likewise based on lived experience, that is just as valid.

Indiscipline, Not Writing, and Filling Up the Well

GAYLE BRANDEIS: "I am a completely undisciplined writer"
In a 2010 interview for *Psychology Today*'s "Creating in Flow" blog, the novelist, poet, and essayist Gayle Brandeis fessed up to a total lack of discipline in her life as a writer:

> I am a completely undisciplined writer. I have no schedule, other than writing when I find slivers of time. My tendency in the past has been to write in big sloppy bursts— I sometimes go for weeks without writing, and then I'm consumed by the need to write and it will gush out quite abundantly (plus I'm a big fan of writing a quick first draft and then using subsequent drafts to shape and hone the work).[6]

Screenwriter and writing coach Jurgen Wolff, commenting on Brandeis's experience, draws out the implication for other writers: "She's so 'undisciplined' that she's managed to write three novels.... So here's to us 'undisciplined' writers, it turns out we're not impostors after all!"[7]

It is hard to imagine a starker contrast than the one between Brandeis's self-account and the advice of O'Connor, Shapiro, and King. The distance between doing all the grunt work yourself by writing three hours every morning to lay textual bricks, and having no schedule and just writing when you're able to snatch some time for it, is immense. The former approach, as we've noted, emerges as the satisfying-sounding principle of inviting inspiration by making space for it to manifest whenever its obscure rhythms make it feel like doing so. But what is the principle involved in Brandeis's counter-account? It's simply this, in her own words, which state a point that is likewise intuitively satisfying: "The non-writing times have been fertile, percolating times, filling the well so it can spill over again."

It is important to place Brandeis's self-account in context. At the time of this interview, she was raising a new baby while coming to terms with the deaths of two close family members, including her mother's suicide, within a single six-month span. She said these events had affected not just her writing life but her daily life at large, so that on those occasions when a moment became available to write, "I often just needed to take that time to decompress and not do much of anything. I'm trying to be gentle with myself and not push myself too hard." At the same time, she said that she did "want to find a better rhythm that creates more space (especially inside myself) for my creative work."

KATE ANGUS: The secret power of not writing

In an essay bearing the provocative title "Maybe the Secret to Writing Is Not Writing?" the poet, essayist, and writing teacher Kate Angus describes a painful experience of writer's block that led her to embrace the cycle of writing/not writing as her creativity's natural rhythm. "For almost two years after my first book was published," she says, "I did not write a single new thing — not an essay, a story, a chapter, an ode, an elegy, nor even a monostich." As with Brandeis's experience, this pause was related to other factors in Angus's life, including the death of a beloved pet, the birth of a new romantic relationship, and a distinct drain on her authorial energy that she experienced from her teaching duties (a phenomenon with which I, too, am intimately familiar).

At first she doggedly tried to keep writing, but it was like chipping away at unyielding ice: "I'd type one or two words and stop and stare at the letters. Then I'd space my cursor backwards, deleting to start again, only to hit another wall. The open document on my computer felt like a white room I was locked inside — no matter how hard I pounded at the walls or how loudly I screamed, I was trapped." Soon she started feeling like a fraud when she stood before her students and had the audacity to talk to them about writing. None of her efforts — taking a meditation course, deliberately courting external deadlines (which she failed to meet), creating alone time for an in-home writer's retreat — proved effective. Inside, she was confused by her failure and longed to return to "the halcyon days when I could take the inchoate feelings, ideas, and experiences that swirled like smoke inside me and alchemize them into words."

And then — the block broke. Like clouds dissipating in the sky to reveal the still-shining sun, "one morning I woke up with the first lines of a poem singing in my head. I got out of bed, sat down at my desk, and began typing; within twenty minutes, I had a new poem." More followed. Angus felt joy but also frustration and fear, since she had not consciously solved the problem and therefore could not be sure if it would recur.

In her essay, she says what eventually saved her was an expanded and transformed view of creativity that invoked the metaphor of crop rotation. Just as fields need to lie fallow from time to time in order to rebuild their nutrient base, so a writer's psyche needs to be allowed to lie fallow from time to time as it recharges through the natural passages of life and experience. Angus quotes the famous line from the Book of Ecclesiastes to encapsulate the point: "To everything there is a season." This is in contrast to the dominant mindset of modern-day business, consumer, and technological culture, which knows and demands only constant production without any sensitivity to the deep cycle of activity and rest that constitutes the natural world and human reality. Angus says she came to realize that it is natural for many writers to alternate between times when words are available and times when they are not. This reframed her former binary understanding of creativity as writing versus not writing. "Even when I'm not writing in the denotative sense of inscribing words on the page," she says, "I'm still writing in a larger sense, as I am doing the necessary work of building up a storehouse of experiences, images, and ideas I will articulate later."[8]

KATHERINE ANNE PORTER: "I Have No Hours at All"

Interestingly and ironically, the case of Flannery O'Connor and her prescriptive three hours at the typewriter every day is paired in *Conversations with Flannery O'Connor* with a counter-example from another prominent writer. One of the items in that book is the transcript of a 1960 panel discussion on southern fiction at Wesleyan College. The moderator's opening question is about the panelists' writing habits. One of the quotes I shared above from O'Connor about her three daily hours comes from the responses. Katherine Anne Porter was also on the panel, and her answer to the same question could not have been more different:

> Well, I have no hours at all, just such as I can snatch from all the other things I do. Once upon a time I tagged a husband around Europe in the Foreign Service for so many years and never lived for more than two years in one place and never knew where I was going to be, and I just wrote what I could and I still do. Once in a while I take the time and run away to an inn and tell them to leave me alone. When I get hungry, I'll come out. And in those times I really get some work done.[9]

Your Core Creative Strategy

To take stock of all this: Flannery O'Connor, Dani Shapiro, and Stephen King all say you have to work hard, put in long hours, shed blood, dig deep, and get covered in mud and filth in order to attract the attention of the muse. According to them, it's only when you have reached your own farthest extremity and exhausted all your own strength that the muse will pay attention. Examples could of course be easily multiplied. There is Steven Pressfield, for instance, who in *The War of Art* talks about generating a kind of magnetic field around yourself, attractive to the muse, through daily dedication. He has expanded on this at his blog, stating that while talent is important, what is more highly favored by the muse is "devotion, dedication, perseverance. When she sees our butts in our seats, she can't help herself; 'Okay, okay, I'll give this poor sucker a couple of ideas today.'"[10]

On the other side of the fence are Brandeis, who says, "I write when I feel like it," and Angus, who rediscovered her creativity by allowing herself long periods of not writing anything, and Porter, who kept no hours and just wrote whenever a moment was available. And they, too, have many peers in their camp.

So what, then, is the upshot, the combined wisdom, the overall point? It is none other than what we started this chapter with: We must each divine the rhythms of our own daemon muse, learning to speak when it speaks and remain silent when it is silent. Or, to put it somewhat poetically in words borrowed and altered from the Bard: *To thine own muse be true.* Your core creative strategy is to discover, through practical experimentation and sensitive attention to what works, the best ways in which your creative daemon needs to have a space cleared for it, and then to forthrightly execute that particular action — or non-action, as the case may be. If writing every day and zealously guarding that carved-out span of time is how you and your inner genius need to work, then run with it, and run hard. If you find through trial and error that you really need to wait until your daemon asserts itself spontaneously by filling you with the desire and ability to write, then run with that instead.

In my experience, both possibilities require serious dedication and self-clarification. It may sound at first blush as if the approach of regular, scheduled work is the one that's all about discipline, and that it is diametrically opposed to the other, which is all about indiscipline. But in fact the latter makes up a deep and serious discipline of its own: that of keeping yourself attuned to your inner states and motivations as you wait for a ripe time to begin writing.

In both cases, the ultimate point is the same: Your muse, daimon, genius possesses its own will and its own ways, and it visits and energizes you as and when it desires. Inspiration comes and goes. Your task is not to generate inspiration, and certainly not to control it, but to channel it, and to do so by whatever means necessary so that when it shows up, you are there to listen, receive, and bring into being what it is intent on giving the world through you.

NOTES

1. Elsewhere, I have illustrated this point with examples, excerpts, and insights from the lives and works of such writers as Philip Larkin, Alice Flaherty, Joe Hill, Amy Lowell, and Victoria Nelson. See Chapter 6 of *A Course in Demonic Creativity*, titled "Divining Your Daimon's Rhythm."
2. O'Connor, Flannery, *The Habit of Being: Letters of Flannery O'Connor*, selected and edited by Sally Fitzgerald (Farrar, Straus, and Giroux, 1988), 417.
3. Rosemary M. Magee, ed., *Conversations with Flannery O'Connor* (University Press of Mississippi, 1987), 38, 47, 62.
4. Dani Shapiro, "On Inspiration," June 25, 2010, *https://danishapiro.com/on-inspiration*.
5. Stephen King, *On Writing: A Memoir of the Craft* (Scribner, 2020), 144, 157.
6. Susan K. Perry, "How a Writer Turned One Rejection into Two Novels,"

interview with Gayle Brandeis, *Psychology Today*, June 21, 2010, *https:// www.psychologytoday.com/us/blog/creating-in-flow/201006/how-a-writer-turned-one-rejection-into-two-novels.*

7. Jurgen Wolff, "So You Don't Write Every Day? Read This!" *Time to Write*, July 8, 2010, *https://timetowrite.blogs.com/weblog/2010/07/so-you-dont-write-every-day-read-this.html.*

8. Kate Angus, "Maybe the Secret to Writing Is Not Writing?" *Literary Hub*, September 24, 2019, *https://lithub.com/maybe-the-secret-to-writing-is-not-writing.*

9. Magee, *Conversations with Flannery O'Connor*, 61–62.

10. Steven Pressfield, "Habit," *Writing Wednesdays*, March 31, 2010, *https:// stevenpressfield.com/2010/03/writing-wednesdays-32-habit.*

6

The Writer's Paradox

Personal Is Universal

Creativity involves a hidden paradox. So does authentic spirituality. Understanding it gives you the secret key to both.

The paradox is centered on a matter of considerable significance for all writers, creators, and spiritual seekers: the relationship between you and others, between your personal depths, desires, and dreams, and the world of otherness in which you perceive yourself to be immersed and with which you perceive yourself to be confronted. How can you write effectively to that, in a way that bridges this gap between yourself and others to forge a link and communicate your vision?

The secret is this: *What is most private and personal in you is also what is most universal.* What is deepest in you is deepest in all people — and in the world itself. The more deeply you look into yourself, the more you find what is most important to everyone. The most private you, "the real you," isn't isolated and alone. Rather, it is your secret point of contact with the whole cosmos. When you speak, write, think, perceive, and act from your deepest, truest self, you automatically speak to other people's deepest desires and concerns as well.

This is the source and essence of creativity on the part of both the creator and the audience. It is also the meaning of spirituality and religion. The composer Richard Strauss characterized it as "the source of Infinite and Eternal energy from which you and I and all things proceed," and he asserted that in addition to being the source of the musical inspiration that he received in his highest moments — which he described as "definite compelling visions, involving a higher selfhood" — it is what religion refers to when it speaks of God.[1] The practical implications are radical.

Real Creative Connection

In making art, music, or literature, the more you base your work on pandering to others to win their attention or approval or to extract their money, the more you miss the mark, because paradoxically the effort to project your motivation outward and shape your work purely for appealing to others serves only to alienate them and make the work sterile. In other words, it has the opposite of the intended effect. Real creative connection with others comes not from chasing after it outwardly but from accessing what is most personal within you and expressing this in some truthful form. "What is most personal is most creative," said the renowned film director Bong Joon-ho, quoting wisdom he remembered gaining from Martin Scorsese. The spiritual teacher Jean Klein said, "Beauty is the same in all," so that "when the artist spontaneously offers his most profound nature and through his talent finds its nearest expression, it awakens in the viewer, the listener, his own profundity."[2]

This means people will recognize themselves and their own deepest concerns in what you honestly express from your most private self.

The psychologist Carl Rogers stated it as a kind of dictum: "What is most personal is most general." He further elaborated: "[W]hat is most personal and unique in each one of us is probably the very element which would, if it were shared or expressed, speak most deeply to others." Rogers said this realization came to him through vivid personal experience, from paying attention to his own feelings when he tried to talk to other people about things that seemed too private to communicate. On such occasions, he said, the opposite of his expectation turned out to be the case:

> There have been times when in talking with students or staff, or in my writing, I have expressed myself in ways so personal that I have felt I was expressing an attitude which it was probable no one else could understand, because it was so uniquely my own.... In these instances I have almost invariably found that the very feeling which has seemed to me most private, most personal, and hence most incomprehensible by others, has turned out to be an expression for which there is a resonance in many other people.[3]

Rogers also said these experiences "helped me to understand artists and poets as people who have dared to express the unique in themselves."

When you apply the same principle in spirituality and religion

— in meditation and prayer, for instance — you find that the only way to uncover what's real in your life is to inquire back into yourself so deeply that you go beyond yourself. Trace your "I" back to its source, and you find not only your own essence but that of your brother, sister, parents, spouse, children, neighbors, co-workers, friends, enemies, strangers, and all people everywhere.

The Whole Energy of the Universe

Recognizing this, and more, realizing it — that is, making it real by feeling its truth and significance, and basing your sense of everything on it, and letting your accompanying actions arise from it — changes everything, not just theoretically but practically, and not just in creativity or religion, but in both. It fundamentally alters how you see, treat, and relate to everyone, because now you realize that in pursuing your own highest fulfillment, your own greatest happiness, your own implanted destiny, whether in creative endeavors or spiritual ones, you are simultaneously pursuing everyone else's.

Equally as important, you realize that in pursuing everyone else's good and fulfillment, you are pursuing your own. "Anyone trying to live a spiritual life," said Henri Nouwen, "will soon discover that the most personal is the most universal, the most hidden is the most public, and the most solitary is the most communal." Nouwen said this fact carries a kind of imperative, because it means our most intimate interiority, our deepest inner lives, are not actually "for" us alone, but are also for others, and in fact for all people. "That," he said, "is why our solitude is a gift to our community, and that is why our most secret thoughts affect our common life."[4]

This is also why Ramana Maharshi, the renowned twentieth-century Indian sage, asserted that "realization of the Self is the greatest help that can be rendered to humanity" — because such self-realization is not egoic self-absorption but a going beyond the self to realize your transcendent identity with that which is the ultimate identity of all people and the world at large.[5] It is a true, deep, and self-evident knowing that, in the words of Alan Watts, "the whole energy which expresses itself in the galaxies is intimate. It is not something to which you are a stranger, but it is that with which you, whatever that is, are intimately bound up. That in your seeing, your hearing, your talking, your thinking, your moving, you express that which it is that moves the sun and other stars."[6] Writers, artists, and sages have always known this, though some have consciously grasped it and articulated it more clearly than others. In keeping with the principle, their very articulations of it are demonstrations of it, communications or transmissions of Truth from Itself to Itself.

If hearing this stirs within you a resonant feeling of recognition and affirmation, you can take this as self-confirmation of the point's validity, a heartful wink and nod being exchanged by Being with Itself through the medium of these words and the vehicle of your and my respective senses of separate identity.

NOTES

1. Arthur M. Abell, *Talks with Great Composers* (Carol Publishing Group, 1994), 86.
2. Jean Klein, *I Am*, compiled and edited by Emma Edwards (Non-Duality Press, 2007), 4.

3. Carl Rogers, *On Becoming a Person: A Therapist's View of Psychotherapy* (Houghton Mifflin, 1961), 26.
4. Henri J. M. Nouwen, *Bread for the Journey: A Daybook of Wisdom and Faith* (HarperOne, 1997), February 23.
5. Ramana Maharshi, *The Teachings of Ramana Maharshi*, ed. Arthur Osborne (Rider Books, 2014), 87.
6. Alan Watts, "Alan Watts: On Being God" (talk recorded in 1971 in New York City at a conference on Western psychological therapy and Eastern religion), *Be Here Now Network*, YouTube video, 1:20:31, December 26, 2022, *https://youtu.be/sZ41zgWHs_I*.

7

Invite the Lightning

The Accident of Inspiration

A well-worn bit of Zen wisdom has it that although enlightenment is a total accident, meditation practice can make you more accident-prone. Nobody is quite sure who first said this, but many members of the modern American Zen community have been suggested. It may have been Shunryu Suzuki. Or Robert Aitken. Or Richard Baker. Or it could have been someone from outside the Zen tradition, such as Rajneesh/Osho or J. Krishnamurti. Or it might have been two or more people in combination. I'm personally inclined to think the mystery of the saying's origin adds to the charm of its insightful expression.

No matter where it came from, what concerns us at the moment is that the same principle holds true when it comes to creativity and the muse. The creative spirit alights on its own schedule. The muse or daemon is under nobody's control, least of all yours. From your and my point of view, its arrival is an accident, a spontaneous, unplannable blessing that is unobtainable through direct effort. But — and here's the thing, the Zen principle in action — through effort, by practicing, by sitting down to work, you can increase your odds of receiving a visit.

Heaven's Gates

Some clarity on the Zen end can be helpfully illuminating for the writing and creativity end. Enlightenment in the Zen sense of a conclusive occurrence of self-realization or spiritual awakening is an "accident" because it is something we cannot attain for ourselves. It has to happen as a moment of grace, something that is simply given to us. It is not obtainable by effort or grasping. It can only be received, not achieved.

This is because enlightenment's nature categorically transcends us. Enlightenment's very essence is a seeing-through of ourselves and the world, a shift in our center of identification. The customary view — which we do not even normally recognize as a view, instead mistaking it for "the way things are" — is that we are separate, individual selves born into a world that preceded us, and that now confronts us as something alien, something outside ourselves. Taoists call this realm "the ten thousand things," the world of multiple separate, individuated beings and objects that bump up against each other in a continual state of competition.

Enlightenment is an awakening to the fact that this conventional view is in effect just a dream. Separation is only notional. It's a kind of feedback loop in awareness. We are like waves on the ocean or whirlpools in a river that have become self-aware as waves or whirlpools and have thus mistakenly viewed themselves as independent beings. Enlightenment is the wave or whirlpool waking up as the ocean or river and realizing it was never separate to begin with.

But then, waking up isn't something a wave or whirlpool can actually do. It doesn't wake up as a wave or whirlpool, because that would imply it is still a separate something that can awaken. Rather, enlightenment is the ocean or stream remembering itself and waking up from the dream of being a wave or a whirlpool. Thus, from the wave or whirlpool's viewpoint, enlightenment is something beyond it, something it cannot effect or gain for itself, since that would only be a perpetuation of the dream of misidentification in separateness.

Hence, it has become common in Zen and other enlightenment-based spiritual circles to speak of enlightenment as an "accident," something that we as separate selves cannot achieve through deliberate effort. We can only receive it, and then only if and when "it" "decides" to happen. As the American spiritual teacher Richard Rose put it to August Turak, the gates of heaven "don't swing in, they only swing out. You can't force your way in. You're only invited. You need some help from the Other Side, because ultimately you can't do it alone."[1]

And yet, paradoxically, spiritual practices — meditation and more — can somehow make us more accident-prone, more liable to receive the happy accident. We still didn't cause it, but somehow we invited it. We made space for it to happen. One of the great twentieth-century Indian sages, Nisargadatta Maharaj, pointed out that although self-realization takes no time in itself, since it is about a timeless reality, in practice most people need some time to "ripen." He said spiritual practices effectively serve as "accelerated ripening."[2] To put it a bit more vigorously, as Rose did to Turak,

"You attack the gates of Heaven with everything you have. Go after it hammer and tongs like your hair was on fire." And even though, yes, you automatically fail for the reasons already given, "in your defeat you surrender, and with your surrender the doors magically swing open."

The Lightning Strike of Grace

All of the above, the very same principle, applies equally to our writing and other creative work. When we sit down to write, if we try to exert control — I mean control in a fundamental sense, trying to do things entirely on our own, to serve as the source of our creativity — we will *ipso facto* exclude the very possibility of transcendence, of becoming a vessel for insights, visions, and truths from beyond the encircling boundary of the ego, the separate I-self that is inherently a contraction of and from the wider whole — in other words, that wave or whirlpool again. But if we instead approach our writing with the attitude that we are opening up to something bigger than ourselves, beyond ourselves, and if we recognize that our efforts and technical skills, combined with our act of deliberate sitting down and opening up, do not produce our true work but instead invite it to happen, we put ourselves in a most fruitful and fateful position.

Steven Pressfield, as mentioned two chapters ago, has powerfully framed the matter like this:

> When we sit down each day and do our work, power concentrates around us. The Muse takes note of our dedication. She approves. We have earned favor in her sight. When we

sit down and work, we become like a magnetized rod that attracts iron filings. Ideas come. Insights accrete.[2]

And then, of course, once the muse has spoken, or while she is still speaking, work again enters the picture, this time not for courting the blessing but for enacting it. As Jean Klein put it, any work of art "is always seen by the artist in an instant, like a flash of lightning, as it surges forth from deep within him. Afterwards he elaborates it, gives it a body and form, in time and space."[3]

To sum up: Both spiritual enlightenment and the touch of your daemon muse are accidents. They are unpredictable moments of divine grace. They are lightning strikes. You can never cause or control such a thing. But you can position yourself where it is more likely to occur. Making a right effort in either realm is like standing at the summit of a hill on a stormy day and holding up a lightning rod. This right effort involves the fusion of control and abandon, effort and relaxation, deliberation and spontaneity, that is the essence of genius and the formula for enlightenment. Strike that balance, find that zone, wait there in that spiritually and existentially liminal space. And see what happens.

The Task Enjoined by Heaven

Here is a personal illustration of the point: As my longtime readers will know, there is no poet in me, at least as judged by the fact that I have never produced a single line of poetry, aside from a few wretched verses that I wrote under duress for English class assignments during my adolescence. Still, one day in late 2022 this thing — the thing below — somehow happened. I honestly can't explain where it came from. All I can tell you is that the circumstances of its origin involved an early morning freewriting session in a kind of creative trance. Afterward, when I looked back at the text on the page, I realized a portion of it was essentially a poem that would reveal itself as such if rearranged into poetic lines. And since the mystery of creativity is our guiding theme here, I thought I would share the result with you:

"The Task Enjoined by Heaven"

There is a voice
Sometimes loud, sometimes soft
It does not care if I hear it

There is a path
Sometimes clear, sometimes not
It does not care if I keep it

There is a flow
Sometimes swift, sometimes slow
It does not care if I feel it

There is a source
Sometimes near, sometimes far
It does not care if I know it

But hearing, keeping, feeling, knowing—
These are all that matter

The title had already suggested itself — spontaneously, without effort, just like the poetic lines themselves — when it occurred to me to look up the phrase "task enjoined by heaven." Any latent sense of a potential daemonic muse involvement in the unexpected appearance of those lines and that title in my unlikely mind was confirmed when I found that the only exact match for this phrase, or at least the only readily locatable one, occurs in the following sentence:

> I pursued my path towards the destruction of the dæmon, more as a task enjoined by heaven, as the mechanical impulse of some power of which I was unconscious, than as the ardent desire of my soul.

The source is Mary Shelley's *Frankenstein,* both the original 1818 edition and the revised 1831 edition. The line occurs very late in the novel, in fact in the last chapter of Victor's portion of the nested narrative, and it expresses his attitude toward the revenge-fueled pursuit of his monster across the European continent and toward the Arctic Circle that occupies the final months of his life. During this journey, he becomes increasingly unmoored from rational consciousness. He feels himself to be surrounded and sustained by benevolent spirits, and he convinces himself that waking reality and dream reality have transposed themselves, so that his daytime pursuit of the monster takes place in a dream, whereas the blissful nocturnal reunions in dreams with his dead loved ones who have been murdered by the monster represent the waking world.

If You Bring Forth What Is Within You
Ms. Shelley's novel has been deeply meaningful to me over the years, assuming the level of one of my core literary texts, a novel

that I return to again and again (as you can already see in this book, given the synergy between this chapter and Chapter Three), and whose themes, world view, philosophical perspectives, and overall tone and energy are part of my foundational outlook. I first read *Frankenstein* in the autumn after my college graduation, when I was experiencing significant psychological turmoil. This meant the emotional agonies endured by both Victor and his wretched creation struck me with an almost preternaturally vivid sense of identification and significance.

A few years later, I took a graduate class devoted entirely to *Frankenstein* and its many literary and philosophical backgrounds and influences, including not only the heady tradition of Gothic novels and ghost stories but the rich trove of additional texts and ideas that young Mary channeled into her hideous progeny, including the ideas about education and human consciousness advanced by her father, William Godwin, and by Rousseau; the alchemical texts and teachings of Cornelius Agrippa and his ilk; and the three books — Goethe's *Sorrows of Young Werther*, Plutarch's *Lives*, and Milton's *Paradise Lost* — that give the unhappy monster his education when he stumbles across them in a forest.

Then I ended up teaching the novel to high school sophomores for six years, which means I can now boast of having read *Frankenstein* cover to cover twenty-one times, fifteen of them out loud with the help and participation of my students. My essay on *Frankenstein* as a kind of parable about the destructive alienation of the visionary creative unconscious from the rational mind under the sway of a scientistic monomania, which appears in my *What the Daemon Said*, expresses some of my deep interests in the story. The upshot is that the archetypal myth of Victor Frankenstein and his monster is imprinted deeply on my literary, philosophical, and spiritual sense of things.

One aspect of the story's multilayered meanings that has always foregrounded itself to me is its rich metaphorical illustration of the potential dangers and difficulties of the creative process. Victor is driven to his act of creation by a ferocious unconscious impulse that he cannot deny. The actual process he employs is both technical and magical, involving a heady fusion of scientific knowledge, skills, and ambitions with visionary and alchemical ones. The end result is likewise as independent and autonomous as the impulse that gave rise to it, representing, in this case, not the purely material-mechanical flesh monster of popular horror entertainment, but the very incarnation of Victor's spiritual double, his literalized, externalized daemon. Because he does not embrace and honor it, they are both destroyed.

"If you bring forth what is within you," says one popular translation of saying 70 in the Gospel of Thomas, "what you bring forth will save you. If you do not bring forth what is within you, what is within you will destroy you." In an interesting variation on the combined promise and warning of this ancient wisdom, Victor brought forth what was within him, but it destroyed them both, because he found himself unable to own or accept it.

Eyes to the Sky

Having endured a sometimes troubled relationship with my creativity, and having found a rich vein of gold in exploring the personification of creativity in the concept — and the vivid experience — of an accompanying muse/daemon/genius, I find the Frankenstein story to be extraordinarily insightful, and also disturbingly cautionary, not only and not even primarily in the ways that have been called out by the legions of readers and commentators who have analyzed it *ad nauseam* as a tale of scientific hubris and the Promethean dangers of "playing God." To me, *Frankenstein*, which Brian Aldiss once astutely characterized as "the first great myth of the industrial age," approaches the status of a master archetype whose meanings can be mined for deep psychological and spiritual application.

So, when the title for the unexpected poetic lines above spontaneously suggested itself, and when I tracked down its origin and found myself reading that resonant passage from late in the story of Victor Frankenstein's descent into a daemonically driven visionary hell, this was simultaneously surprising, confirming, and unsettling. In other words, it evoked a heady cognitive-emotional state of intensified synchronistic sensitivity, which, as I have learned and relearned over the years, is typical of encounters with the numinous guidance that lies beneath and behind the veil of the individual ego mind.

As for what those lines might mean, I can only say that they're quite meaningful and helpful to me as a tool for spiritual course correction, and that I take no credit for having written them. The lightning struck, and I happened to be standing there waiting at the peak of a hill where a storm was brewing. Or maybe it wasn't a hill so much as a Gothic tower, inside of which a monstrous patchwork body lay shrouded in sheets in a scientist's laboratory, waiting for the primal spark of life to come shooting down from the heavens and animate it. Whatever it was, for the sake of your creativity and your purpose in life — to put it redundantly, since those two are really one — I encourage you to join me in keeping an eye on the weather.

NOTES

1. As quoted/recounted by August Turak in his 2023 memoir *Not Less Than Everything: One Man's Quest for Spiritual Enlightenment* (Clovercroft Publishing, 2023), chap. 3, Kindle.
2. Nisargadatta Maharaj, *I Am That: Talks with Sri Nisargadatta Maharaj*, trans. Maurice Frydman, rev. and ed. Sudhakar S. Dikshit (The Acorn Press, 1999), 195.
3. Steven Pressfield, *The War of Art: Break Through the Blocks and Win Your Inner Creative Battles* (Black Irish Entertainment LLC, 2002), 108.
4. Klein, *I Am*, 3.

8

Embrace the Unknown

The Fantasy of Control

"What we hope for is to proceed from the known to the known. We are not enthused about abandoning the known and engaging the unknown."[1] This insight on spiritual awakening from the late nondual writer/teacher Robert Wolfe applies equally to writers. Our default comfort zone is to feel as if we know what we're doing when we start putting words on the page. We commonly assume that the order of progression for producing a completed work is something like this:

1. Have an idea.
2. Start writing.
3. Develop the idea in the direction that you imagined and expected when you began.
4. Write "THE END."
5. Experience a fulfilling sense of creative accomplishment. And maybe publish the thing and receive some money.

As anyone who has gone at this writing thing for any appreciable length of time can tell you, that assumed approach reveals itself as pure fantasy at a frequency of somewhere between ninety-nine and one hundred percent of the time. In fact, what it envisions is pretty much the obverse of how writing really works. We only maintain the fantasy because it provides a comforting illusion of knowledge and control — comforting, that is, to our separate self-sense, our ego self, whose sense of things is to be mistrusted automatically and on principle, since it represents the precise opposite of what is really the case in our lives and the universe.

Beyond and Within

The actual creative process is much more convoluted, obscure, and mysterious than the tidy one above. For many or most of us, that means it is also much more uncomfortable. We are far less at ease with actively not knowing than we are with indulging the illusion of knowledge and control. We don't like it when the thing we're working on, the idea we are attempting to manifest, takes on a life of its own and begins leading us along in a rush, or perhaps at a crawl, amid an enveloping gloom that prevents us from seeing more than a few steps or words ahead. This gloom is, of course, the darkness of living and writing into the dark that we considered in this book's introduction. We feel ill at ease when, instead of conceiving an idea and then working in a rational and organized manner to produce something from it, we realize that an idea has seized us and is now dragging us headlong into the shadows of the unforeseen.

But our discomfort doesn't really matter in the end, because whether or not we like it, that's how it works. Moreover, that darkness of the unknown and unforeseen is where the real fulfillment lies, for it is there that your writing becomes a conduit for something bigger than you to announce itself through you. It is in the encounter with this darkness that you enter the mode of selfless creativity that, as A. D. Sertillanges put it in his classic book *The Intellectual Life*, "makes us interest ourselves in what is beyond us and yet has taken up its abode in our consciousness."[2]

Fictive Dreams and Footprints in the Snow

And so we are back to Dean Wesley Smith again, and his call to write our novels — and by extension do all our creative work — without a preconceived outline, simply trusting in both our creative mind and the intrinsic power and coherence of narrative to carry us through and plot a right course. We are with Ray Bradbury, who urged us to remember that *"plot* is no more than footprints left in the snow *after* your characters have run by on their way to incredible destinations. *Plot* is observed after the fact rather than before." This is the same Bradbury who said most of his books and stories had come as a complete surprise, the result of the fact that in his early twenties he had serendipitously "floundered into a word association process in which I simply got out of bed each morning, walked to my desk, and put down any word or series of words that happened along in my head," after which some massaging of this material would result in a story.[3]

John Gardner called it following the "fictive dream" and averred that "this and nothing else is the desperately sought and tragically fragile writer's process: in his imagination, he sees made-up people doing things — sees them clearly — and in the act of wondering what they will do next he sees what they will do next, and all this he writes down in the best, most accurate words he can find."[4] Gardner was talking about writing novels, but his point holds for writers of nonfiction as well, not to mention for poets, artists, musicians, and people involved in any kind of creative work at all. As iterated upon by Gardner himself, as well as Bradbury, Smith, Michael La Ronn, and others we could name, it also applies more broadly to our entire lives, and to the life of the world itself.

I speak from personal experience. Each of the essays in my *What the Daemon Said*, for instance, emerged out of my life in an unexpected way. So did the stories in my *To Rouse Leviathan*. For that matter, so did the opportunity to collect all those stories and essays into books, where their various interlinkages, as inhering in and emerging out of the "coherence of my self" that William Stafford talked about, could become evident. I didn't plan any of that. It just happened. The "plot" of those books' creation, and also of the surrounding context of my life during the twenty-odd years when those stories and essays came out of me, can only be read in reverse, like footprints left in the snow after my life ran on its way to incredible destinations.

Submit Yourself to an Unknown Fear

So, the question arises: If you are a writer, as you work on your current book, story, essay, poem, or script, are you trying to force it to be something that fulfills a preconceived notion? Are you locking it — and yourself — into a comforting but ultimately futile and sterile illusion of rational knowledge and certainty? Or are you letting the thing reveal what it inherently wants to be? Are you allowing something beyond your conscious grasp and intentions to be infused in it? Are you letting it tell you where it wants to go and how it wants to get there — in short, what it really, deeply is? Are you allowing the same thing, the same unfolding of mystery, in your wider life?

H. P. Lovecraft famously said, "The oldest and strongest emotion of mankind is fear, and the oldest and strongest kind of fear is fear of the unknown." We encounter that fear — hell, we invite it — each time we pick up our pen, or sit down at our keyboard, or wake up in the morning.

In *All's Well That Ends Well*, Shakespeare said:

They say miracles are past; and we have our
philosophical persons, to make modern and familiar,
things supernatural and causeless. Hence is it that
we make trifles of terrors, ensconcing ourselves
into seeming knowledge, when we should submit
ourselves to an unknown fear.
(1.3. 891–896)

Don't let the ancient fear of the unknown lead you to "make trifles of terrors" in your writing and thereby prevent potentially transcendent and transformative truths from speaking through your pen. If you will follow the fictive dream; if you will write and live into the dark; if you will take an interest in the thing from beyond that has taken up an abode in your consciousness; if you will submit yourself to that unknown fear — if you will do these things, you may well find a miracle waiting on the other side of the darkness that you dread.

NOTES

1. Robert Wolfe, *Living Nonduality* (Karina Library, 2009), 325.
2. A.D. Sertillanges, *The Intellectual Life: Its Spirits, Conditions, Methods*, trans. Mary Ryan (The Newman Press, 1960), xv–xvi.
3. Ray Bradbury, *Zen in the Art of Writing* (Bantam Books, 1990), 139, 85 (Bradbury's emphases).
4. John Gardner, *On Becoming a Novelist* (W. W. Norton & Company, 1999), 120.

PART TWO

The Flashpoint of Silence

Utter stillness is death for the sense of self, it is the demise of the future of promise; it is to sprawl point-blank on the moment. What it might portend, one must admit one does not know. In that empty space lies the possibility of creation which is not merely a continuation.
— ROBERT WOLFE

I have often regretted my speech, never my silence.
— PUBLILIUS SYRUS

9

Surrender to Stillness

The Whisper of Inertia

We begin this second part of the book with a confrontational and perhaps uncomfortable question, one that I bring to you from my experience as a writer over many years: Are you ever tempted to abandon all your creative projects? Let them collapse? Maybe even let your whole outer life crumble as you sit there silently and watch it all burn down? Is there ever an inner spiritual call to do this? If so, is it valid? Should we assent to it? Or is this desire instead your enemy: the energy of self-defeat, the siren song of your lower self, a function of negative self-image and defective mental/emotional programming? Could it even be the voice of some evil demon that we ought to recognize and resist, a spirit of destruction working to overturn and undermine us?

The call to sink into inertia and give everything up is a question and a temptation that has suggested itself to me many times over the course of my life. The peculiar nature of my mental-emotional makeup apparently renders me susceptible to such thinking. I have repeatedly experienced moments when it becomes apparent that what I am seeking through my creative efforts and actions is in fact a sense of final fulfillment in which I will not feel the need to do such things anymore, but will instead feel free simply to exist, to be, to sit in silence. (Remember what I said in Chapter Two about both fulfilling and transcending the creative impulse.)

Being reasonably well read in the literature on creativity, I'm self-aware enough to ask at such moments: Is this simply a manifestation of Resistance (a term and concept to be examined in Part Three)? Or is there something valid about that inner murmur that urges me to let go, sink down, and give blissful assent to the dream of entire rest?

Several times over the years, at moments when a sense of mutual resonance with a fellow writer or creator has led me to feel comfortable enough to share what can feel like my shameful secret, I have described this experience in words. And these moments of self-disclosure have pointed up an interesting fact: I'm not the only one. My sense of isolation in this experience is actually a function or manifestation of the writer's paradox that I mentioned three chapters ago, the ironic revelation that what we think is most private and peculiar about us is actually the most universal. Other people, other writers, have encountered the same inner sea change. They grok it with gusto, including not only the sudden — or sometimes lasting — desire to drop everything and go silent, but the same sense of combined dread and relief that accompanies it. Maybe you are one of them.

Naturally, a recurrent feeling this powerful and long-lived in my experience has made itself known in my journals. For thirty years I kept a private journal that served as one of the chief external repositories of my inner life. It was there that I learned the sound of my own voice, the nature of my fascinations, and the style and mode of writing that was natural to my self-expression in words. I brought this centered knowledge of myself to my public writing as well. And then, unexpectedly, my private writings became grouped with my public ones when much of my journal was published in two volumes.

There are many entries in its pages dealing with this long-running, ever-returning, always attractive and seductive and convincing call to quit everything and retreat into a cocoon of blessed, blissful silence and stasis. The following example is a case in point that shows me grappling with the pull toward absolute inertia. Maybe you'll find something in it that resonates with your own experience. Note that when the entry mentions "the mummy book," this refers to *Mummies around the World: An Encyclopedia of Mummies in History, Religion, and Popular Culture*, which I edited for an academic publisher, and which was published in 2014. When I wrote this journal entry, I was deep into the process of that book. And when the entry mentions "the paranormal encyclopedia," this refers to *Ghosts, Spirits, and Psychics: The Paranormal from Alchemy to Zombies*, which I edited for the same publisher, and which was published in 2015.

SATURDAY, APRIL 27, 2013 – 6:26 A.M.

I have various responsibilities in the realm of form that have been given to me, and various ones that I have deliberately taken on. Such as the mummy book. Now I'm being pressed to fulfill the interest I expressed in editing the paranormal encyclopedia. And I have let it lie undone (the prospectus/proposal) for two months. Mummy work has been sporadic as well.

A recent reading in *My Utmost for His Highest* shows Oswald chiding those who always wait for inspiration before they will act, for, as he puts it, if we all waited until we felt like it before doing something, then some of us would never do anything at all. Pick yourself up by the scruff of the neck, he says, shake yourself off, and get going.

But of course he also rightly advises in many other places that when you're toiling in the trenches with no present sense of vision, inspiration, or guidance, you must follow the "heavenly vision" and the remembered inspiration of those mount-of-transfiguration moments. This entails that at least once you actually saw the vision clearly, and that you now remember it accurately and retain the sense and understanding of its import and where it's leading.

But what if that hasn't happened?

Or what if the vision itself has been of a kind of stasis, a falling away of all action because it's all a castle built on sand — this whole creaking structure of egoic self-image and an externally constructed life situation? Eckhart Tolle sitting on his park bench for two years while his promising academic career collapses. Jesus and his conventionally useless and titanically failed life. Ramana Maharshi reclining on his couch.

Is there ever a real call just to cease all action and let structures crumble, as overt "failure" blooms all around?[1]

As I said, when I wrote those words I was deep into editing *Mummies around the World* and conceiving the proposal for what became *Ghosts, Spirits, and Psychics.* I was also working full-time as a college writing center instructor and English faculty member, even as I was managing all the responsibilities of a husband and family man. Amid this swirl of competing calls and obligations, the desire just to let go of everything was a constant whisper, a silently thrumming inner suggestion that hovered on the margins of my awareness and sometimes converged toward the center like a warm syrup of psychic Novocaine.

And then, with exquisite timing, in walked the above-quoted passage from the works of Oswald Chambers — the early twentieth-century Scottish preacher, teacher, and missionary, who would later become the subject of my doctoral dissertation — to challenge me. If you're personally familiar with the inner call to silence and stillness, then you will understand me when I say that Oswald's words felt like both a welcome motivational prod and a threat to my introverted fantasy of being completely free of external obligations and therefore free to relax and sink into nothingness.

The call to action, to shake off the down-dragging gravity of stillness, represents the norm, the base level, the default attitude in a culture of hustle like America and a collective civilization of relentless activity like the one that we maintain right now on planet Earth. As I see it, this means the opposite attraction to stillness needs to be recognized and honored as a counterbalance to an otherwise unhinged devotion to constant work and movement.

Some words from Robert Wolfe in his booklet titled "Elementary Cloudwatching," which he created from a year's worth of his private journal entries, convey the mood of this inner stillness as well as anything could:

> Civilization and stillness — quiet, inactivity — do not go together. Civilization is a continual process of choices; stillness comes without choice. There is nothing which can be done to create this stillness. It is not something which is to be acquired; it has no value as currency. It is, put another way, priceless.
>
> One must relax, to breathe this stillness. Not just the body: the mind, the psyche. One must relax ambition. Ambition and stillness are not compatible. There is no ticking of the clock here. There is no effort in stillness."[2]

"There is no effort in stillness." Exactly. Therein lies the attraction, the reason we crave it.

Digital Echoes

The relationship between this inner call to stillness and the hyper-world of digitally interconnected chatter and restlessness that envelops so many of us nowadays is well worth pondering. In late 2022 I launched my "Living Dark" newsletter. Not long after that, the online platform that I had chosen for it, Substack, launched its new "Notes" feature, representing the company's first foray into social media. I began experimenting with it and found it rather enjoyable, since it enabled me to share short ideas, quotes, links, one-off thoughts, and other items that would not add up to a full newsletter post but could still serve to connect me with readers and foster enjoyable communication and interactions.

However, as I observed the enormous surge of launch-week activity on Notes from all kinds of writers, I also found some thoughts arising within me about the importance of using technologies like that with care and self-awareness. Then I discovered that others were thinking the same thing. Only a week after the launch of Notes, a handful of Substack writers announced that they had experimented with it and decided not to use it going forward, both because it was unmoderated and because it represented yet another temptation to scatter their energy and attention into the digital wind. One writer said she wanted to avoid the inherent gravitational pull of social media toward converting herself and her writing into products to be advertised and used for gaining attention and subscribers.

I feel these concerns deeply. Social media carry the inherent risk of colonizing our minds with the virus of hustle and self-promotion. For that matter, so does all online writing, with its potential for delivering instant feedback in the form of clicks, likes, and comments that can tell us how many people are reading our work and how they are reacting to it.

This means it is necessary to make a deliberate practice of focusing on the writing itself as an end and a value in its own right, because the other alternative, which is not really so much an alternative as a consequence, is to give free rein to your egoic-addictive craving for attention and validation, and thus become its slave, and more than that, its carrier. What is needed, in other words, is a Buddhist-like freedom from attachment to the fruits of one's actions. But this is a practice and an ideal that may stand in a position of intrinsic conflict with likes, reposts, and eyes on subscriber counts.

The Weight of Words

As the above matters percolated in my psyche, something else came to mind, a unit of wisdom from a lovely but mostly forgotten American television series from the early 1990s. The series lodged in my memory when I first watched it, and I have found it resurfacing from time to time over the years whenever my attraction to retreat and stillness is ascendant.

Key West ran for a single season on the Fox network in 1993. It was about a man named Seamus, enjoyably played by Fisher Stevens, who wins the lottery, abandons his blue-collar job, and flees his former life as a factory worker in New Jersey to head south to Key West, where he hopes to fulfill his lifelong dream of living as a writer like his idol, Ernest Hemingway. But what he actually ends up doing is becoming a reporter for a tiny local newspaper while learning to navigate his way through a town full of bizarrely eccentric characters.

A storyline in one episode has Seamus incessantly pestering his editor, Roosevelt, to give him a weekly column. Roosevelt is a blind man whom the show frames as a kind of caustic wisdom mentor for Seamus's hero's journey. In one key exchange, Roosevelt asks Seamus what he thinks he would write about in his column. "Oh, you know," Seamus replies. "Observations. Insights."

Roosevelt says, "What makes you think anybody gives a diddly about your observations and insights?"

Seamus, obviously caught off guard, pauses a moment, then

says tentatively, "Well..."

To which Roosevelt replies, "Good answer."

For all of us who conduct a life of sharing ideas, information, and "content" online — and really, for all of us creative types who have the audacity to put words out into the world for other people to read and react to — Roosevelt's question is well worth pondering. What makes you think anybody cares about your words, your observations and insights, your vision and ideas? For many people, your "value add" to their daily experience may not seem all that valuable. In light of this, and as stated above, what's needed is to do the work for its own sake, as arising out of an authentic inner need, conviction, desire, or direction for doing so.[3]

There was also another key moment in *Key West* that rewards serious reflection by all of us who would undertake to write publicly and expect other people to read it, and also by all of us who must negotiate the relationship between writing, speech, and silence. It occurs at the end of the second episode, which is the one in which Seamus, having initially resisted the newspaper job because he has higher literary aspirations, realizes he needs to accept it. This comes after he has freaked out for the entire episode because he has learned the shocking news that nearly all his lottery winnings are gone, which means his irresponsible life decisions are now poised to come crashing down on him. He needs steady work. So he returns to the newspaper office at night and tells Roosevelt that he will take the job. Roosevelt gruffly tells him he isn't ready to write for the paper because he doesn't know enough. "I don't need to write," says Seamus. "I just need to be near the writing. I need to be around it." He ends up accepting a menial job at $4.00 per hour. Roosevelt tosses him a broom and says, "Get to work."

Seamus begins sweeping the newsroom floor. After a moment, Roosevelt, listening to the sound of the broom, chuckles and says, "You're gonna learn something, newshound." Seamus, still sweeping, nods and says, "Yeah." Then Roosevelt leans forward in his chair and asks Seamus what he has learned.

Seamus pauses, looks at Roosevelt, and opens his mouth to speak. But then he thinks better of it, shuts his mouth with a slight smile that's partly forlorn and partly peaceful, and returns to sweeping. Roosevelt nods and says, "Keep sweeping, newshound. You may be a writer someday."

Like Seamus, all of us who are saddled with the desire to write these days may need the wisdom to shut up sometimes and just sweep the floor, just devote ourselves to some useful work, however conventionally menial or minor, while we detach from our inner glory hound and voluntarily undergo a period of spiritual and psychological detoxification, a time of listening in silence to the world around us and within us. If we are truly meant to write, then anything of value that might come from doing it will arise out of that kind of inner attitude and outer practice, not from a frenetic grasping for validation via shares, click counts, comments, recommendations, reviews, or other forms of external validation.

Additional wisdom comes from another television character who similarly received much of his spiritual training by wielding a broom. During my adolescence in the 1980s, I exulted in reruns of *Kung Fu* on WGN, which I would watch each Saturday evening after auto-recording them on a VHS cassette earlier in the day while I traveled an hour away to nearby Joplin, Missouri, for martial arts lessons. The series' protagonist, Kwai Chang Caine, was one of my heroes. I was particularly entranced by his pseudo-Buddhist utterances, which awoke a deep fascination within me. One of the most potent of these, stating a point that I came to ponder frequently, was, "If one's words are no better than silence, one should keep silent." At the time I didn't know that he, or rather the scriptwriter, was actually quoting Confucius. But it doesn't matter who first said it. I cannot think of a more helpfully countercultural attitude to adopt in today's world. I also cannot think of a more deeply beneficial and healing attitude for writers in particular, including me, to adopt. Are our words at any given moment really better than silence? Do they outweigh the enduring value of silence as the ultimate teacher and revealer of subtle truth? Can we cultivate the awareness to keep this question near, and the will to act — or, as the case may be, not act — on the honest answer to it?

The Flashpoint of Stillness

The following lines are excerpted from several pages of spiritual teacher/writer Art Ticknor's book *Solid Ground of Being*:

> Few of us are natural philosophers. We have to see that other interests are peripheral before we turn whole-heartedly to self-inquiry... as holding the most likely hope for satisfaction of our deepest longing....
>
> Everyone has a strategy they're pursuing to get what they want out of life. It may be conscious or largely

unconscious. Becoming conscious of your strategy is a step in the direction of waking up.....

Getting serious is the equivalent of getting honest with yourself. Are you serious about finding the truth of your existence?... Gautama Buddha apparently got serious when he sat down under the Bo tree; Jesus, when he spent 40 days in the desert....

You can't force yourself to get serious. You basically have to run out of other options. As Winston Churchill quipped or complained about Americans... "[They can] always be counted on to do the right thing — after they have exhausted all other possibilities."

When you recognize that your hunger won't be satisfied by even the highest external games (for example, the metagames of art, science and religion in DeRopp's [sic] Master Game), then the only possibility for satisfaction lies within... the game of discovering who you truly are.

Ticknor then quotes Steve Jobs:

"People think that focus means saying yes to the things you've got to focus on. But that's not what it means at all. It means saying no to the 100 other good ideas that there are. You have to pick carefully. Life is brief, and then you die, you know?"[4]

So: If you, like me, have felt yourself powerfully drawn throughout life to those "metagames of art, science, and religion," as described by Robert S. de Ropp in his classic 1968 book *The Master Game*, how much of your immersion in such things has always been, and still remains, a distraction from your life's true goal?

I personally go through repeated cycles of attachment/detachment, immersion/distancing, even obsession/repulsion, in my writing and creative pursuits. Usually the times when I feel most distanced from these pursuits coincide with the times when I feel the most real, the most open, the most centered. That's when I zero in on my real calling — when the impulse to write, compose music, read books, or engage and communicate at all dies down to a slow simmer, tending toward full stop.

Which is all to say that my public creative output has always felt like it's imbued with a kind of half-life, a built-in period of decay, after which it will be lights out, total silence. And that will be when I have really grabbed hold of the golden ring.

The same may be true of you. Maybe we are all writing — and composing, speaking, religion-ing, art-ing, science-ing, working, whatevering — in search of the flashpoint of stillness, when we will realize that we don't have to do it anymore, and that we don't even want to do it anymore, because we have finally waked up from the dream and found the thing-in-itself, the absolute, the ultimate noumenon of self-knowledge that we were always seeking obliquely through mediated means. "I have no reason to write and yet I do it," says Wolfe in *Elementary Cloudwatching*.

There is nothing more satisfying than to sit here for hours, attentive to the beauty in the day wrapped around me. I have no motivation to take my eyes from the satin blue sky, the scrubby green hills, the sunlight and shadows of the oak tree, and to focus them instead on a lined-paper pad — and yet something motivates me. The writing appears without any real effort on my part, but I am relieved when I can again turn away from it.[5]

And yet there is an even further level or layer to this cycle. To preview what we will look at in more detail in Part Three, the thing I keep circling back around to is the fact that, notwithstanding Wolfe's experience, it is specifically the effort-filled approach to writing and creativity that tends to generate this desire to give it all up. The effort to create from the standpoint of the dream of separate personhood causes stress because it is motivated by the desire to accomplish or gain something. But the dream itself, this sense of separate perspective, is just spontaneously arising. It is here without any effort. So the ideal, I keep re-realizing, is not a silence and stillness that appears as such on the surface, but the silence and stillness of recognizing, identifying with, and resting in the pure being-awareness that I actually am, and from that stand-point, watching whatever wants to happen just happen within the appearance. This is the ultimate creative state, one in which there is no effort and no resistance to what either appears or does not appear. But it takes a long time for most of us to recognize that state, let alone realize it, as in making it real in our lives.

NOTES

1. Matt Cardin, *Journals, Volume 2: 2002–2022* (Sarnath Press, 2023), 236–237.
2. Robert Wolfe, *Elementary Cloudwatching: 31 Meditations on Living without Time* (Karina Library Press, 2013), "Sunday Matinee." Wolfe

created this booklet, which he originally gave the subtitle "Contemplating the Meaning of Living in the Moment," near the end of a three-year period in the 1970s when he lived alone in a camper van in the California Redwoods.

3. On this count, I direct you to my *A Course in Demonic Creativity*, especially the fourth chapter, "Getting to Know Your Creative Demon."

4. Art Ticknor, *Solid Ground of Being* (TAT Foundation Press, 2014), chaps. 9 and 10, Kindle.

5. Wolfe, *Elementary Cloudwatching*, "No Reason."

10

The Crossroads of Spirit and Art

The Creator's Inner Struggle

The hard question at the start of the previous chapter — the question of how to understand and handle the recurrent desire to abandon your creative work and just sink into silence — now leads us to a hard truth about a popular assumption involving creativity and spirituality. It is common to think these two go together, to view them as pleasantly and naturally compatible. Many people enjoy believing that heightened or deepened spiritual experience is mutually supportive of enhanced creative flow. Offhand, I can think of at least half a dozen books that either touch on this premise or are mounted forthrightly upon it. Some of them rank among my personal library of favorites.

But is the claim they advance accurate? Is it unqualifiedly true? Is there perhaps another view, a counter-experience, a contradictory truth? Is it possible that, contrary to popular belief, the two activities, experiences, or modes of being that we call "creativity" and "spirituality" — the desire for which is so commonly lodged within the same person — are inherently antagonistic? Might they even, to an extent, be mutually exclusive?

Sara Maitland, the British novelist, certainly thought so. Or rather, she stumbled into this conflict in a circumstance that she had thought would produce the exact opposite, a situation and environment where she had expected to find her creativity energized instead of enervated. As she recounts in her sublime memoir, *A Book of Silence*, sometime in mid-life, having established herself as an author and feminist activist, and having raised her children, she reached a point where she felt overwhelmed by the constant noise and demands of modern society. This led her to leave her existing life behind as she went on a quest for silence. The experiment took her many places, including the Sinai Desert, the Scottish hills, and the Isle of Skye, where she rented a remote cottage and spent forty days in total solitude. Eventually her search for locations that resonated with her spiritual goals led her to the picturesque valley of Weardale in County Durham, England, which had both a reputation for tranquility and a historical connection to hermits and anchorites. She rented a small cottage and ensconced herself in its silence and seclusion, using it as a place to focus on both her writing and her contemplative practices.

However, she soon found that, to her surprise and dismay, things were not unfolding as she had hoped. Her account is both poignant and riveting as she describes a profound case of writer's block that raised fundamental questions about the relationship between writing and spirituality:

I noticed something shocking. I had come to Weardale for
four conscious reasons: to study and think about silence,

to find out if it was delightful for me, to deepen my prayer life and to write better. I was indeed doing and enjoying all the first three, but I was not, in fact, writing. Or to be more precise, I was not writing any fiction and certainly not of the kind I wanted to write.... The desire to write, to tell stories that pull my thoughts and emotions together, has been something that I have lived with and found integral to my sense of well-being, even of identity, for as long as I can remember. Now quite simply stories did not spring to mind; my imagination did not take a narrative form. I had in a peculiarly literal way "lost the plot." I found this disturbing.

Maitland says that, in keeping with the common notion that silence and solitude are good for writers, she had assumed "that I could go and lurk up on a high moor, put in the disciplined practice of contemplation and meditation, and thus become both a better, more prolific imaginative writer and more safely and intensely engaged in the life of prayer." However, reality was now proving her wrong, and this led to a painful new question:

Is it possible to have both — to be the person who prays, who seeks union with the divine and to be the person who writes, and in particular writes prose narratives? I was very much aware that I have always believed that silence, and particularly silence in "nature," was supposed to stimulate both artistic creativity and religious spirituality. That was not what I was experiencing.

This all began to lead her to the realization that she could not write and be silent at the same time. It also pressed upon her the sense of a dilemma and an accompanying decision that she had never thought she would have to make:

> I began to feel that this means, or might mean, that I had to make radical choices about who I chose to be. Could I be happy to give up writing? Could I be contented with a more active and businesslike kind of religious practice? The answer to both questions, most of the time, was "no."
> I had a problem.[1]

As I have said, the same dilemma, the same tension between silence and spirituality on the one hand and writing and creative action on the other, has occupied an important place in my own life. The following circuitously unfolding line of thought, though not expressed in the first-person language of personal confession that Maitland used, and that I employed myself in the last chapter, can still be accurately understood in that sense. It articulates an understanding of these matters that, emerging out of my experience and reflection, has proved helpful and meaningful. I suspect that aspects of it may speak to your own experience, too.

The Demon of Ego

Recall Rilke's famous line about being afraid that if he submitted to psychoanalysis, it might drive out not only his demons but his angels. His point seems to have been that exorcising his devils, his hangups, his neuroses and other nominally negative psychological issues, would also exorcise the angels of creativity that drove his poetry.

Now factor in nonduality, the apex of spiritual awakening, whose promise and premise is to recognize the nondual (undivided, "not two") nature of reality. This is the basic nondual insight. Nondual awakening is the ultimate recognition and deliverer of the oneness, the unity, and the attendant freedom from fear, anxiety, and conflict, both outer and inner, that so many spiritual seekers crave.

Nonduality includes and hinges on, and in fact basically is, the realization that one does not really exist as a separate self. The core nondual insight is that the very sense of being a separate individual, an ego, is a kind of dream being had by the one Self. The experience of you-plus-universe, self and other, subject and object, is really just a kind of hypnotic trance in which the sole Self, the Ground of Being, the Supreme Identity, as Alan Watts sometimes called it, is imagining itself as divided.

Thus, awakening from the dream of ego constitutes "the end of the world." It dissolves or sees through the self-world divide. After this, there is no more separate self. There are no more "ten thousand things." There is just "thou art that," and "that" is all — including the dream of separation, which continues to play itself out like a movie or virtual reality with "you" as one of the fictional characters.

This being the case, and returning to Rilke's terms, isn't the real "demon" in fact your very self? Isn't the separate ego the archdevil — or at least the dream of one — that rules and gives rise to all the rest, the whole teeming realm of separation, confusion, conflict, and suffering?

And so, therefore, wasn't Rilke fundamentally correct, but in a way that requires us to reframe his insight a bit? Isn't it not so much your angel but your demon — perhaps an ultimately artificial distinction — that is the source of creativity, both the flow of ideas and the felt drive to manifest and communicate them in the dream world of form?

Becalmed on the Sea of Being

In *Living Nonduality*, Robert Wolfe shares his letters to a correspondent in prison. One in particular is pertinent to the tension between creativity and spiritual awakening. Apparently Wolfe's correspondent had been doing some self-writing, maybe keeping a journal for self-exploration and catharsis concerning painful life experiences. Wolfe comments:

> Yes, writing about the maelstroms of our life can be an effective way to purge the repressed energies. But this is to dwell on the past, which is devoid of reality. Better to spend the time considering whether that fictional character of the past is not a fictional character of the present. To whom did these things happen, and by whom were they precipitated? What is the source of all activity, including self/Self-examination? You made the appropriate surmise, in my opinion: "They need to be let go of." And even the self (subject) that would be parted from them (object). As you said, "Those things are not me." No "thing" is. Neti, neti. "Not this, nor this."...

Every action is ultimately pointless; when ultimate Truth is realized, it is clear that "only your mind moves," as a Zen parable has it.[2]

Consider: Is it not the case that to dispel your ego entity — by waking from it and seeing that it was never really there to begin with — is likewise to dispel the maelstrom of "your life," thus leaving you becalmed? Except there is no "you" or "your." There is now just the infinite, placid sea of being.

The logical upshot is that if you are a creatively driven person who cherishes your desire to write or otherwise create, and at the same time you are a person who feels drawn to spirituality, a wise bit of advice may well be: "Beware." Someday you may find that you have been pursuing intrinsically antagonistic ends and undercutting yourself at every turn. You may be frustrating yourself on both sides, the creative and the spiritual. In seeking "spiritual awakening," you may not be enhancing your creativity but undermining it. And reciprocally, in seeking to cultivate your creativity, you may be undermining your search for spiritual awakening. Contrary to popular belief, these two may not be mutually supportive.

It is illuminating to note that on at least one occasion when Rilke talked about the danger of exorcising his angels along with his demons, he did so in the context of reflecting on a long-simmering idea that had taken hold of him: to give up writing. Specifically, he said:

I know now that analysis would make sense for me only if I were truly serious about that strange thought at the back of my mind — *no longer to write.... Then* one might have one's devils driven out, since in ordinary bourgeois life they are really only bothersome and awkward anyway, and if by some chance the angels left with them, well, one could view that too as a simplification and tell oneself that in one's new, one's next occupation (but which?) there would certainly be no useful place for them.[3]

It may be for you as it was for Rilke: that the "strange thought" of no longer writing hovers and murmurs in the back of your mind, and that heeding it could simplify your life. You may find yourself one day making a choice.

Or more accurately, it may be that a choice will one day happen, but when it does, it will not be, nor will it feel like, a choice at all. Or at least not one that you as an autonomous agent have made. To slightly revise a metaphor put forth by David Carse in *Perfect Brilliant Stillness*, one day you may find yourself approaching a great wall, and after much searching you may find a gate in it. You may step through this gate, and then turn around to find that there is actually no gate at all. There never was. Nor is there a wall.[4]

Nor, for that matter, is there a "you."

Divining the Deep

I hasten to add that, as I mentioned at the end of the previous chapter, a deeper kind of creativity may reveal itself at some point, maybe in the wake of conventional creativity's death, or maybe during the agonizing struggles leading up to it. What you have always thought of as "my creativity" may well have been an egoic affair all along, a masked search for personal fulfillment through praise and self-satisfaction, perhaps the outworking of a compulsion neurosis or some other psychological complex or nominal defect in the psyche. If and when this egoic glitch goes away or is seen through, either because it is "healed" on its own level or because it is recontextualized by an awakening to a higher level, the latent creative force that gives rise to the dream of the world itself might become activated through and within the dream form of you.

Note the present tense: the creative force that *gives* rise to the world, not that *gave* rise to it. The creation of the world is always occurring right here in the present, as a perpetual arising in the eternity of this now moment. If that somehow becomes linked to (the dream character of) you — as in, for example, the experience of encountering and interacting with your daemon muse, the darkly enigmatic bearer and emblem of your creative purpose and whole life destiny — all bets are off. Stupendous and even explosive creativity may occur. I will say much more about this in Chapter Fourteen.

For now, suffice it to say that this spontaneous flow of primal and primary creativity may not look like anything that you or anyone else ever imagined or expected. You may find yourself the carrier or conduit of, in the words of the biblical Paul, "what no eye has seen, nor ear heard, nor the human heart conceived.... what has been hidden from the foundation of the world." Which, again, is all the more reason to beware.

If there is a way through this apparent stalemate between

awakening and creation, it may lie in seeing them not as enemies but as two faces of the same mystery. The question then becomes how to live when the pull of silence and the call of the daemon are both present, both insistent — and perhaps, in their deepest essence, not really separate at all.

NOTES

1. Sara Maitland, *A Book of Silence* (Counterpoint, 2008), 189, 190, 192, 193.
2. Wolfe, *Living Nonduality*, 265.
3. Rainer Maria Rilke, letter to Lou Andreas-Salomé, January 14, 1912, in *Rilke and Andreas-Salomé: A Love Story in Letters*, trans. Edward Snow and Michael Winkler (W. W. Norton & Company, 2006), 185 (Rilke's emphases).
4. See David Carse, *Perfect Brilliant Stillness: Beyond the Individual Self* (Non-Duality Press, 2005), 74.

11

Nonduality and the Daemon

From Demotivation to Divine Purpose

Two of the most deeply felt fascinations that have gripped me over the years — and they're honestly not just fascinations but full-blown obsessions, the chief orienting points of my life — are the matters of spiritual awakening and life purpose or calling. You could also call them, as indeed we have been calling them in this book, *nonduality* and the *daemon*. The former has involved finding out who I really am and what the world really is, in the knowledge of what we are not. The second has involved coming to understand the specific energy that moves me, my reason for being, what I am supposed to be doing with the life experience that I have been handed. Obviously, these two are not unrelated. In fact, as I have cultivated a deepened engagement with them over time, it has become apparent that they are not two but one. They are different aspects of the same thing.

Once when I was doing some meditative early morning reading, I came across a line in a book that illuminated this matter as well as anything I have ever read. The book was *Full Stop! The Gateway to Present Perfection* by the now retired/former nondual writer and teacher John Wheeler. The chapter was titled "Non-Duality and Social Reform." It presented a dialogue between Wheeler and one of his readers/students. The latter expressed a fear of losing interest in the world and arriving at a state of total demotivation if the nondual understanding were really to sink in. On the one hand, the person said he/she felt a desire to work for increased personal and societal spiritual awareness, saying, "I want to write and create art that pushes the envelope, ruffles feathers or even simply offers simple truth in the service of cultural evolution." On the other hand, this desire was accompanied by the fear that experiencing nondual awareness — the realization that the common notion of being a separate self in an objective world of multiplicity is just a kind of mirage or projection, and that your real identity is the awake spaciousness of absolute Being itself — would undercut the creative desire and produce a state of becalmed apathy and detachment.

This resonated deeply with me, as it echoed things that I, too, have considered, mulled over, and encountered. The question is compelling: What truly is the relationship between nonduality and the daemon? As we asked in the previous chapter, is there an inherent antagonism between waking up and remaining active in the world, if waking up reveals the nonexistence of the self that one has cherished and identified with? Does spiritual insight entail worldly quietism and relinquishment of creative drive, an automatic dampening of the daemon muse? Or is there a subtler relationship?

On that early morning when I was alone with Wheeler's book, I was delighted to find that his response to the question of creativity versus quietism both amplified and clarified my own apprehension of the matter and encapsulated it in an understated way that fulfills both of its aspects.

Here is the key passage, with its primary sentence — a statement that constitutes a veritable recipe for living — italicized by me:

> [Nonduality and creative action in the world] are not contradictory, so do not make a duality of them. *Find out who you are and naturally serve your allotted function in life as it comes up to do.* In the final non-dual view, there are no individuals nor any external world to help. Even viewing this way is a product of dualistic conceptualising. So again, you are mixing up different subjects or levels of discourse. There is no conflict between knowing who you are and the other admirable goals you are mentioning. The conflict is coming in within the mind, which is imagining them to be antagonistic.[1]

"Find out who you are and naturally serve your allotted function in life as it comes up to do." These words stopped me in my readerly tracks and kept me sitting there for several minutes in meditative silence while their implications unfurled. Both halves of the sentence function together, with each corresponding to one wing of a central concern: "Find out who you are" refers to nonduality. "Naturally serve your allotted function in life as it comes up to do" refers to the daemon.

Here is how this plays out to bridge the gap between absolute presence and relative purpose with a living understanding of both:

Find Out Who You Are

Do this not as an exercise in abstract conceptual knowledge, but on direct present evidence, meaning the evidence of first-person-hood. Who and what are you, really, as the aware presence to which the entire combined sensorium and mental/imaginative world of the bodymind are appearing? Who and what are you at this moment that witnesses even this question as just another appearance or experience that has come up and will soon pass on?

Everything is an appearance to you. Everything comes up and goes away, even the experience of being you, as seen in your disappearance every night and reappearance each morning. You are the pure substratum of being-awareness out of which and in which the experience of the world, and of yourself as a separate presence in it, arises and subsides, appears and disappears, rises and sets. This is verifiable right now, without moving a muscle or changing anything about what is appearing. Whatever the basis of everything is, you are that.

Serve Your Allotted Function

The wave on the surface of being that is this appearance of you-plus-world has a natural momentum to play out, a given direction and set of qualities. Relative to the projected dream of being a separate identity, this natural momentum and allotted function can be understood and engaged as a character and a calling, a dharma and a destiny, a given (not chosen) set of talents and predilections, personality and preferences, drives and desires, along with external circumstances that seem to constellate inevitably in tandem with these inner qualities to reveal a discernible theme. This all emerges, in other words, as a daemon, *your* daemon, a specific-to-you energy or magnetism, influence or intelligence, that shapes your life both subjectively and objectively, revealing and evincing the pattern, the blueprint, that you were born to realize and fulfill.

Your daemon is the invisible color frequency that has saturated your life since you first opened your eyes on the world. It is the sub-aural bass note that has been thrumming below the threshold of conscious awareness in every aspect of your hearing since you were in the womb. It is both peculiar to you and larger or deeper than you, rooted in Being itself and serving as the bridge between you and the Absolute. And when this daemon is fulfilled, when the sun of your self is ready to set, nothing has actually changed, because — to switch metaphors freely — the wave was never anything but the ocean all along. How to live? How to know what to do with yourself in this life? Find out who you are and naturally serve your allotted function as it comes up to do.

The Self, the Daemon, and the One

I wrote the explication above for myself and to myself in a heady rush on that morning when I was reading Wheeler's book, right in the wake of encountering his lucid and lovely formulation of how to live. Then I shared it on social media. Someone who read it asked, "From a non-dualistic perspective, how can there be both a daemon and a self?" It's a good question, which is why I preserve it here, along with the answer that I wrote for the questioner to frame the relationship between nonduality and the daemon in a different way.

The separation in question — between oneself and the daemon

— is all a projection, something that is real on its own level in relativity, but that resolves into just the One Self in the absolute. The dream of being a separate person is experienced on the subjective side as having multiple levels. Or really and basically, there are just two levels, though many systems of psychology have tried to get more subtle and complex than that. These basic levels are the conscious and unconscious minds, the ego and the submerged psyche. One could add the physical body, too, but that is just part of and inseparable from the ego. The unconscious, broadly framed and conceived, is both the daemon and the muse. And it is fused at its roots to the wider realm of Being itself. It is through the unconscious daemon muse that the conscious egoic self is connected back to its source, its ever-present primal origin in the absolute.

And as I said, this whole structure is ultimately a karmic wave rippling across the surface of being. It's also a magic eye picture that, when you look at it long enough, drops away into a depth you had not recognized before, even though it was right there all along for the seeing.

Speaking of seeing, as we move into the next chapter, we will see that this unity reveals itself in the most ordinary moments, even in something as simple as how we read, and in the unexpected ways a passing encounter with words can open onto the silence beyond them.

NOTES

1. John Wheeler, *Full Stop! The Gateway to Present Perfection* (Non-Duality Press, 2012), *https://johnwheelernonduality.wordpress.com/wp-content/uploads/2020/04/full-stop-wheeler-john.pdf*, 306–307.

12

Breaking the Spell of Words

Reading, More or Less

It was an early Sunday morning in December, well before sunrise, and I was engaged in my customary post-meditation ritual of drinking two cups of coffee while reading and annotating spiritual and other books, essays, and articles. On that particular morning, one of the items I had queued up to read was an online article that was presented in that familiar format where only the first few paragraphs were initially visible, accompanied by a "Read More" button at bottom that I could click to see the rest. I clicked it and finished the article. Then I scrolled back to the top, and as I did so, I came across a section heading that I hadn't noticed during my reading. It said, "Read Less." I thought, "Oh, I missed that part!" and paused to read it. Then I realized my silly error: The heading was actually the "Read More" button, now transformed into its opposite, enabling me to hide the "more" text if I wanted.

I laughed at my little mistake. But then I paused and noticed something important: The article was on a spiritual topic, and when I came across what I thought was a missed section about reading less, a little spark of pleasure ignited within me. I instantly, tacitly assumed that I was going to read some advice about cutting back on the number of things I read and/or the time I devote to reading, advice about reducing reading to a more focused activity and a less profligate, distracting, and dissipating one. I assumed I was going to imbibe some wisdom about letting go of the FOMO associated with seeing an endless stream of apparently cogent and worthwhile books, articles, essays, and blog posts flooding my field of attention and leading me to employ an app, or browser tabs, or PDF printouts, or email folders, or some other tool or tech to save all those things for later, resulting in an infinite backlog of unread material piling up not just digitally but psychologically, like an expanding gallery of accusing stares lodged in the back of my mind. That morning, as I stumbled across what I briefly mistook for a subsection titled "Read Less" in a spiritual article about the wisdom of letting negative emotional and cognitive responses to life's contingencies serve as valuable opportunities for spontaneous healing and change, I felt a little surge of hope at the thought that what I was about to read would speak some healing peace and spaciousness to me.

When I laughed, it was not only because I recognized my mistake, but because I realized I didn't need any such section of any such article to give me permission. I am already able, I already have standing permission from the universe, to let go of any felt pressure to keep up with the endless tide of books and other teeming texts that wash up on the shore of my world. I already know all about this. And I hope you do, too.

I know that my self isn't in those books and essays. For much of my life, I read books and other things in a frankly desperate, craving way, hoping to find The Answer to the problem that was given to me when I was born. It took several decades and college degrees, and the cultivation of a hyper-developed intellect stocked with more texts than the Library of Congress and the Library of Alexandria combined, for me to arrive, not through reading but through realization, at the recognition that the answer is not in a book at all but in the one who reads books in search of the answer. The same principle also applies, of course, to all the other objective/external things — jobs, personal relationships, possessions, places, reputation, and more — that we use to deceive ourselves by projecting onto them and into them the sense of a primal goal to be achieved or answer to be found. I have placed stock in each of those things myself at various times. But books have always been my preferred repository.

So my accidental/imagined admonition to "Read Less" was not strictly necessary. But apparently I needed to be reminded of it, enough so that I inadvertently manufactured an occasion for it to happen.

The Limits of Language

This experience plays into a significant realization: Words are not real. Or rather, words are not reality. This is a core truth, a foundational axiom, that has special importance for writers and others for whom words are their stock-in-trade. And even beyond that, this intrinsic gap between words and reality is crucially important for those of us who are drawn to the religious and spiritual deployment of the texts that we call "scriptures."

The point is stark and simple: No authentic religious or

spiritual scripture is really understood unless you share the in-spired inner state from which it was written. If you approach a scripture — Buddhist, Christian, or any other — for religious/spiritual purposes, and you take the text as truth itself, you're letting it drive you further into the very state of ignorance or delusion that you are ostensibly seeking to escape, remedy, or transcend by reading it. This is not the "fault" of the scripture, but of the way you approach it. Spiritual words are pointers, not the thing they point to. By forgetting this and confusing the levels, you corrupt the scripture by inadvertently trying to make it be, say, and do what it can never actually do, what it was never *meant* to do.

Truth transcends language. You can see this in something as simple as an apple. The object itself is not the word "apple" but rather the experiential reality of a real-world fruit, and of the tree from which it emerged, and of the entire planetary and cosmic ecosystem of which it is a particular point of manifestation. You cannot eat the word "apple." The word is just a signifier. The reality it gestures toward categorically transcends it. If this is how it is with something as simple and mundane as an apple, then how much more so is it the case, and how much vaster is the gulf between language and reality, when it comes to words about ultimate truth?

So that's all what we might call the "negative" side of the matter, the recognition of what words cannot do, whether for religious and spiritual literature or anything else. But on the other end of the same recognition, there is a luminous positive complement: A scripture comes alive when something shifts within you, and suddenly you realize you are no longer seeking truth in it or from it, but resonating perfectly with it and perceiving the words as linguistic expressions and confirmations of what you presently already know firsthand, beyond the words themselves, as the living reality of your own deepest being.

In fact, any words become a scripture when this happens, when you see that resonant truth reflected in them. The only difference is that the texts commonly labeled as such, if they are really worthy of the label, were written directly from a vivid state of inspiration that arose from the clear seeing of the truth itself, so that they serve as particularly potent expressions of it.

Moreover — and here the point widens out to encompass matters of importance to all writers, whether or not they are nominally interested in religion and spirituality — the same principle of transmitted vision encoded by someone in and from a state of direct knowing, transmitted via the medium of the word, and then received and decoded by someone who shares the same knowing state, actually applies to all writing. All the greatest, most powerful writing is a case of transmitted vision, of one person making it possible for another to see and share their inner state — a bridging of the gap between separate subjectivities, revealing the substratum of shared being that lies beneath, behind, and before. And the most wonderful thing is that such clear seeing can actually be aided by the clarifying prompts of the words themselves, assuming they are not mistaken for the actual truth.

In an essay that I wrote titled "On Transmitting Artistic and Spiritual Vision" and self-published in a little ebook titled *Transmitting Vision*, I said the following:

When we consider the capacity of language, particularly in its poetical or otherwise artistically deployed form, to alter, shape, shade, and create states of mind and affect, what we're really considering is a convergence of art and, for lack of a better word, spirituality. We are also highlighting a key distinction in the way language can affect us in both arenas. This distinction is between the transmission of *visions* (plural) and the transmission of *vision* (singular). By the former I mean thoughts, concepts, stories, images — all the actual content that can be communicated by language. By the latter I refer to the much deeper impact that language can have by working a change not just on what we think and see with our mind's eye, but on *how* we think and see. In art and spirituality, the most profound effects come from the alteration of a person's basic outlook and worldview, his or her fundamental cognitive, emotional, and perceptual stance toward self and world. This is the level at which visions become vision, and an entirely new way not just of seeing, but of being, opens out from one's first-personhood.

The exact nature of this type of transformation or awakening, apart from but related to its intimacy with language, has been articulated in various ways throughout history by, among others, religious visionaries. Not all transmissions of vision are of the specifically religious sort. But reflecting on the religious kind can be helpful in clarifying the experience and reality in question.

For me, and also, I assume, for you, these truths are operative in both life as a writer and life as a reader, which are of course not at all separable from each other (see Chapter Two), and which in the end amount to the same thing. Whether we are reading or writing a scripture, story, poem, or anything else, what counts is clear seeing, depth of vision, intensity of insight, and potency of the energetic inspirational charge poured into the words and communicated across the gulf between apparently separate minds and selves. As long as we remember that the words are not truth, and can never be the truth, but can only gesture toward it with greater or lesser degrees of artistry and effectiveness, then we are free to read them and write them with gusto, using them on either end of the authorial relationship as magical spells, incantations, an art form of interpersonal alchemy. Importantly, this kind of magic does not enchant us or put us to sleep. Rather, it wakes up. It reveals us to ourselves by transmitting a vision of truth from one person to another, and by transmuting the author-reader relationship into one of shared transcendent vision and true communion of souls on a plane beyond language.

Silence Between the Lines

At the risk of invoking irony, let me relate this to a book. After all, books, like everything else, can serve as valuable pointers to truth even though they can never be or embody the truth themselves. They only represent a siren song if we let ourselves take them that way.

Around thirty years ago, when I was fresh out of college, I was captivated by the book *Journey of Awakening* by Ram Dass, which I found in a bookstore in Springfield, Missouri — probably Waldenbooks in the Battlefield Mall, where I spent so much of my life that I may as well have installed a cot. Though it is hard to single out a portion of this lovely little tome that moved me more than any other, the author's words about making your life lighter by simplifying it, along with the personal illustration that he used to drive the point home, may have been the most memorable. Ram Dass said:

> As you enter quieter spaces [through meditating] you will see how clinging to desires has made your life complicated. Your clinging drags you from desire to desire, whim to whim, creating more and more complex entanglements....
>
> If... you run around filling your mind with this and that, you will discover that your entire meditation is spent in letting go of the stuff you just finished collecting in the past few hours.... This encourages you to simplify your life.

He recommended that we keep track of the specific kinds of mental distractions that keep coming up when we observe our minds, since these will be different for each person. He also described the benefits of doing this:

> You will easily see what you must clean out of your closet in order to proceed more smoothly....
>
> Each time you lighten your life, you are less at the whim of thought forms, both your own and others'. It's as if you have built a world based on the thoughts of who you seem to be.... Each time you give up an attachment to a thought form, your world becomes that much lighter and clearer.

To illustrate, he described his former relationship with music and the way it had changed as he introduced meditative space into his life. His words are piercingly resonant with my own experience of both music and books:

> I recall that as a Harvard professor I had FM in my car and stereo in my office and home; I was constantly surrounded by music — even with a speaker in my bathroom. In addition there were paintings on all the walls and decorations on my car.
>
> Slowly, as meditation changed my perception of the universe, I started to crave simplicity. I placed objects on the walls that reminded me of higher possibilities: pictures of beings who were in higher consciousness, symbols of this consciousness, and art that represented it. I found that I was beginning to appreciate the silence and was content to enjoy a few pieces of music or art thoroughly rather than fill every space with sound and with imagery.
>
> At times, I even felt the total contentment that comes from sitting in silence in a purely white room.[1]

As I said, this has always stuck with me, and I think of it fairly often. This is because, in addition to the interesting fact that the passage's final line stands as perhaps the perfect complement to Pascal's famous observation that "all of humanity's problems stem from man's inability to sit quietly in a room alone," I personally know whereof Ram Dass was speaking. Three decades ago, in my early twenties, I could sense its wisdom, but apparently there was still a karmic load of obsessiveness over books and reading that had to be played out in this life. I intensely felt that I understood and agreed with his point, but my addiction to reading simply wouldn't let up.

If you ever run into any of my old friends and coworkers from Glen Campbell's former music theater in Branson, Missouri, in the mid-1990s, ask them about my practice, which I later found was kind of legendary at the theater, of reading books while directing the video portions of Glen's live shows. I mean I did both at the same time. As I called the shots, communicated with my camera crew through the headsets, ran the video switcher, and called up and ran prerecorded video segments on the IMAG screens at the requisite points in the show, I was also reading books by Huston Smith, Alan Watts, Allan Bloom, H. P. Lovecraft, Theodore Roszak, and more, holding them open with my left hand right there on the video switcher console. ("I have had much trouble getting along with my ideas," Carl Jung said in his autobiography. "There was a daimon in me, and in the end, its presence proved decisive. It overpowered me, and if I was at times ruthless it was because I was in the grip of the daimon."[2])

At my next job, at Missouri State University, I essentially wall-papered my office with printed out quotations from various world mystical/spiritual texts and traditions, along with quotes from my favorite poets and poems, such as Walt Whitman's "Song of the Open Road." I mean there were scores of them — maybe hundreds. I liked to read these quotes while taking breaks from my electronic media production work. I also burned with yearning for the spiritual freedom and insight they expressed, but that I was unable to feel for myself. Thinking back on it now, I see how much those literal walls of words became not so much windows on spirit as a prison for — or rather a prison of — my mind.

But over time, mercifully, that all changed. My relationship to reading and other clinging obsessions lightened up as clarity arose over the emptiness of the self that was obsessed. As with Ram Dass's relationship to music, this transformation has also changed the nature of what I am drawn to read, along with how I relate to it and what I derive from it. Sometimes, as with my "Read Less" experience, I am brought to reflect on these very changes by passing circumstances.

And what about you? Do you feel the pressure of a mounting backlog of unread books and things that you think you want to read and/or ought to read? Are your bookshelves — and your inbox, web browser, and reading apps — piled high with accusing stacks? If so, are you really obligated to take on that pressure? To be complete and fulfilled, to be who you already are, the truth behind your persona, do you need to read anything? Do you even need to finish reading this book, or even this chapter? Can anything that I say set you free? Or do I only, in a sense, erect more bars for this prison with every word I write?

Remember in the movie *Network* when Howard Beale yelled at his prime-time network television audience to wake up from the collective trance of TV and turn off their sets? "This is mass madness, you maniacs!" he shouted. "In God's name, you people are the real thing! We [on television] are the illusion! So, turn off your television sets. Turn them off now. Turn them off right now. Turn them off and leave them off. Turn them off right in the middle of the sentence I'm speaking to you now. Turn them off!"

I feel like doing a riff on that here. Stop reading these words. Close the book. Back away and step out of the cage of your verbal mind, the narrow-necked Zen bottle with the full-grown goose inside. Notice the wider reality of what is beyond the trance of these words, including your real self as the ground of it. Stop reading these words right now. Stop this very second. Stop right in the middle of the sentence I'm

NOTES

1. Ram Dass, *Journey of Awakening: A Meditator's Guidebook* (Bantam Books, 1990), 109, 110–111, 111.
2. C. G. Jung, *Memories, Dreams, Reflections*, rev. edition, ed. Aniela Jaffé, trans. Richard and Clara Winston (Vintage Books, 1989), 356.

PART THREE

The Axis of Creation

Work of the eyes is done, now
go and do heart-work
on all the images imprisoned within you.
— Rainer Maria Rilke

The Tao does nothing, yet nothing is left undone.
— Lao Tzu

13

The Illusion of Obstruction

I BEGIN this third and final section of the book by summing up and extending the themes explored in the first two. And I do it in a pointedly personal way, since these are themes that have emerged out of my own life and experience.

Over many years, and through the course of my creative unfolding as a writer and a human being, the idea of the daemon muse has become one of my life's focal points. This has evolved and extended itself in a similarly organic way to link up with my long-running focus on nonduality and final spiritual awakening. Also involved, and perhaps topping it all off, is the driving desire to understand the relationship between words and silence, activity and passivity, motivation and demotivation, writing and not writing, effort and rest, that occupied us in Part Two. This all culminates here, in these final three chapters, which articulate an approach to creativity and life that draws these strands together.

We launch on a nominally negative note by defining the primordial enemy of creative work and life purpose. In the subsequent chapters, we further develop and delve into this theme by deeply

interrogating this creative enemy in order to explore what lies behind it, subsisting in an inner/outer, creative/spiritual space that
merges into the deep realms in which, as Jacob Needleman powerfully put it, we "open within ourselves to the great flow of fundamental forces that constitute the ultimate nature of the universe,"
such that we come to exhibit "the quality of human action that allows
the central, creative power of the universe to manifest through it."[1]

Understanding the Enemy

When Steven Pressfield laid out the concept of Resistance in his
classic guide to creativity, *The War of Art*, he gave quintessential
expression to a primordial negative and even demonic power in
human experience. Half or more of the book is epitomized by the
saying, "Know your enemy." The remainder is epitomized with
equal pithiness by the complementary injunction to "know your
ally." The term "Resistance," with its capital R indicating Pressfield's savvy strategy of personifying it as an actual, living adversary,
quickly entered the lexicon of many writers and artists, becoming
a standard part of our working vocabulary and conceptual arsenal.

Pressfield says real writers, in contrast to wannabes, know that
writing itself isn't hard. Rather, the hard part is actually sitting
down to do it. "What keeps us from sitting down," says Pressfield,
"is Resistance."[2] He devotes the first section of his book to defining,
delineating, and exposing Resistance in its various guises and
manifestations, and then the second section to describing his philosophy of "turning pro" — that is, taking a serious, practical, and
ruthlessly businesslike attitude toward your work — as a way to
combat this enemy.

Resistance, Pressfield explains, is the factor within your own mind that keeps you from doing your work, following your calling, and fulfilling your purpose. He illustrates and elaborates with many cogent and pungent images and insights, such as the following:

- We experience Resistance "as an energy field radiating from a work-in-potential. It's a repelling force" whose "aim is to shove us away, distract us, prevent us from doing our work."
- It is internal to us but feels as if it comes from outside. It is "the enemy within."
- It is a cunning liar that "will tell you anything." It will come up with any and every reason, rational or irrational, to keep you away from your work. "Resistance," Pressfield says bluntly, "is always lying and always full of shit."
- It is also monstrous: "Resistance is like the Alien or the Terminator or the shark in Jaws. It cannot be reasoned with.... It is an engine of destruction, programmed from the factory with one object: to prevent us from doing our work."[3]

When you just can't get started on a project, or when you rationalize your way out of even trying, you're dealing with Resistance. When you give in to discouragement, fear, or self-doubt, you're giving in to Resistance. When you let your critical editor's mind stifle the spontaneity of your primary creative mind, you're agreeing with Resistance. When for any reason you fail to start or finish a work that you initially felt called to do with a sense of motivation or even inspiration, a work that you truly, deeply knew and still know that you're meant to do, you have come up against Resistance, and you have let it defeat you.

Its most insidious trick is to masquerade as your own thoughts. You think those reasons that keep coming to you for why you can't or shouldn't start/finish the work are all sound, sensible, and valid, but that's actually Resistance undermining you by doing a psychic ventriloquist act with your inner voice.

Pressfield says much more about Resistance than what I can cover in this brief summary. He talks about it in relation to such things as procrastination, self-medication, sex, fundamentalism, self-doubt, the desire for stardom, and your choice of a mate.

But perhaps the most important point he makes, for practical purposes, is that "Resistance is infallible." What he means is that this negative force can actually guide you to the work you are supposed to be doing. How can it do this? Simple:

> Like a magnetized needle floating on the surface of oil, Resistance will unfailingly point to true North — meaning that calling or action it most wants us to stop from doing.
>
> We can use this. We can use it as a compass. We can navigate by Resistance, letting it guide us to that calling or action that we must follow before all others.
>
> Rule of thumb: The more important a call or action is to our soul's evolution, the more Resistance we will feel toward pursuing it.[4]

If you are perhaps thinking this sounds a lot like an alternate articulation of Marcus Aurelius's famous statement that "the impediment to action advances action," so that "what stands in the way becomes the way" — advice transformed by Ryan Holiday into "the obstacle is the way" in his bestselling book of that title — you're not wrong. In fact, you're quite right. This insight, which effectively inverts customary thinking by reframing the enemy's role and hijacking its energy to aid and advance our own ends, represents a truly perennial point of wisdom. Pressfield and Holiday are drawing gold from the same ancient mine. (If any further evidence were needed, there's the fact that Holiday's book comes with a glowing blurb from Pressfield right on the cover.)[5]

Unveiling the Ally

Significantly, in this realm of the psychically autonomous — of those forces in the psyche that are extra-egoic and therefore feel to your conscious self as if they are separate from "I," possessing independent agency apart from your conscious will — Resistance is not unopposed. There is another primordial power, an obverse energy, that works against it. This is of course the daemon muse that we have been talking about throughout this book. Pressfield talks about it in the third section of *The War of Art*, titled "Beyond Resistance: The Higher Realm." This is the realm of the aforementioned ally, where the muse, the daimon, and the genius live, those angelic energies that guide and empower us in the work we are meant to accomplish. Just as there is a force that we can fruitfully personify as our enemy, Pressfield says there is also a force that we can fruitfully personify as our friend:

[W]hen we sit down day after day and keep grinding, something mysterious starts to happen. A process is set into motion by which, inevitably and infallibly, heaven comes to our aid. Unseen forces enlist in our cause; serendipity reinforces our purpose.

This is the other secret that real artists know and wannabe writers don't. When we sit down each day and do our work, power concentrates around us. The Muse takes note of our dedication. She approves. We have earned favor in her sight. When we sit down and work, we become like a magnetized rod that attracts iron filings. Ideas come. Insights accrete.[6]

Pressfield's presentation of Resistance, and also his handling of the muse, and really the entirety of *The War of Art*, is so trenchant, bracing, and deadly straight to the point that you really need to read it yourself if you haven't already. I'm not going to burn up any more space by summarizing the remainder of its content, especially since it's a brief book that you can easily read in a single sitting if you want to, though for maximum appreciation and impact I think a more effective approach would be to read it over three days, devoting one day to each section.

Rather than restating for Pressfield what he can more ably tell you himself, my point here is to establish, as background, his essential and eminently practical concept of Resistance as a preface to laying out my own insights into the experience of grappling with and coming to understand the nature of this force on a profound level. The next chapter explains how Resistance is actually a ruse, a con, a sleight-of-hand, because at root it is the source of both an artificial — because egoically driven — desire to create and an accompanying, complementary sense of desperate inability to do so. It generates, and in fact it is, its own problem, which it then fools you into claiming as yours. When you dissolve this deception by seeing through it, you find yourself plugged into the infinite creative energy that gives rise to the cosmos itself.

NOTES

1. Jacob Needleman, introduction to *Tao Te Ching*, trans. Gia-fu Feng and Jane English (Vintage Books, 1989), xiv, x.
2. Pressfield, *The War of Art*, front matter.
3. Ibid., 7, 8, 9, 10.
4. Ibid., 12.
5. Reading the full "obstacle is the way" source quote in its original context is helpful. It comes from Marcus Aurelius's *Meditations*, book 5, section 20. Holiday used the 2002 translation by Gregory Hays, which renders the passage like this: "In a sense, people are our proper occupation. Our job is to do them good and put up with them. But when they obstruct our proper tasks, they become irrelevant to us — like sun, wind, animals. Our actions may be impeded by them, but there can be no impeding our intentions or our dispositions. Because we can accommodate and adapt. The mind adapts and converts to its own purposes the obstacle to our acting. The impediment to action advances action. What stands in the way becomes the way." (Marcus Aurelius, *Meditations*, trans. George Hays [The Modern Library, 2002], 60) I like the translation by Robin Waterfield, too, in which the final lines are as follows: "The mind can adapt and alter every impediment to action to serve its purpose; something that might have hindered a task contributes to it instead, and something that was an obstacle on the road helps you on your way" (Marcus Aurelius, *Meditations: The Annotated Edition*, trans. and ed. Robin Waterfield [Basic Books, 2021], 111).
6. Pressfield, *The War of Art*, 108.

14

The Flow of Creation

THIS CHAPTER'S angle of approach is idiosyncratic. It comes at the subject of creative Resistance and how to understand it — and how to see through it to the deep source of all creativity — from a perspective that is highly personal and, I think, unconventional. Rather than focusing on practical aspects of dealing with Resistance and creative block in daily work, I address the matter at the foundational level of the psyche, where these hindrances are attached to the very drive to write itself. (Amusingly and/or ironically, it took me nearly a month to write this thing when I originally developed it as an essay that I published in *The Living Dark*. During that time, I sometimes felt defeated by it and considered giving up. Apparently my personal Angel of Resistance has a sense of humor.)

I note this up front simply to alert you to the fact that the progression of thought in this chapter follows its own internal logic. I fashioned it from things that came to me in private journal writing several years ago. Banking on the paradoxical principle examined in Chapter Six — that what is most personal and private is also what will connect most deeply with other people when shared —

I trust that my thoughts here will speak to some things that are meaningful to you. But if what I describe about Resistance indicating a potential falseness in one's base creative motive sounds foreign, I hope you will at least remain open to the argument and follow it to the end, where maybe we'll come together again.

The Hollowing Out of the Creative Drive

The concept of Resistance struck me so deeply when I first encountered it around 2009 — seven years after the initial publication of Pressfield's *The War of Art*, and six years after the publication of my first book — because I had already been grappling with the firsthand experience of it for many years. As reflected intermittently throughout my journals, in the early aughts I began to encounter a pointed, piercing sense of block on my creative output, both authorial and musical. It took an exceptionally insidious form, because it was not just a matter of feeling sterile, incapable, bereft of ideas, or otherwise prevented in any of the usual forms from starting or finishing a piece of work that I really wanted to pursue. Rather, it was an attack on my very sense of wanting to pursue any work at all. It felt like a draining of my core motivation, a hollowing out of my creative drive. Simply put, I was hit by wave after wave of felt uselessness, the powerful, spontaneous feeling and accompanying notion that writing a story or essay, or composing a song, or sometimes even writing in my journal, was flatly, absolutely, wearyingly, gallingly pointless.

Being attuned as I am to the wavelength of philosophical reflection, I both inhabited this experience — even as it also inhabited me — and studied it. I strove to understand it without rejecting it out of hand, even as I suffered from it. And it was the suffering that kept me from simply accepting it. I could easily see that there were no reasons to consider it flatly wrong, disordered, or suspect out of hand, because the question of whether creative output was a necessary and automatic good had some intrinsic validity. The thought that nothing really, ultimately mattered about my creative ideas and projects, either the completion or the abandoning of them, seemed to have real merit, theoretically speaking. And yet the living fact that I suffered from a sense of inner suffocation and mounting despair at my growing roster of creative misfires, stillbirths, and wholesale failures to launch took a toll. The pain of it kept me digging for answers, for clarity, for some position of stable, defensible affirmation, whether of my creative drive's authentic uselessness, in which case I was off the hook, or its authentic value and meaningfulness, in which case I was off course and careening into personal disaster.

To put some flesh on these bones, here are three representative excerpts from my journal, spanning eighteen years and demonstrating that this has been a chronic issue. I share them on the chance and assumption that aspects of them will resonate with things you have encountered in your own creative journey.

From Wednesday, April 4, 2004, around 1:30 p.m.:

What is this that's going on inside me? I might equally well ask what it is that's *not* going on inside me. This feeling of emptiness, of numbness (sometimes), of deadness, of spiritual lethargy, is about as profound as I think it can be. There is absolutely nothing coming up from the depths inside me, no creative impulse like the ones that have always been with me since childhood. Or rather, whenever an idea does spontaneously occur, when some idea or train of thought takes off on its own regarding a movie, song, or story that might be created, or whenever that generalized, nonspecific desire to "create something" comes over me, something inside dismisses it — simply, effortlessly, instantaneously, as if the idea had never really occurred. I could say that "I" dismiss it, except that it doesn't feel like that anymore. It feels as if the dismissing happens on its own with just the tiniest bit of willful help from me, which exists merely in the form of acknowledging the uselessness of the idea, or rather of acknowledging the uselessness of trying to follow it, work it out, or manifest it in some completed, tangible form.

Next, an entry from exactly nine years later, on Tuesday, April 9, 2013, 6:22 a.m.:

The effort of writing has come to seem an insurmountable barrier that defies and repels me even before I begin. I experience a desperate lack of conviction about the entire act, process, result, and value of writing itself.

The merest thought of writing my own stories, and the thought of the blind-foraging mountain range of epic suffering and discouragement that it inevitably demands, complete with near-fatal disruptions to the stability and peace of my inner state, daily life, and personal relationships — all the wild-swinging moods of elation and depression, and the half-passionate, half-desperate moods of withdrawal and self-absorption — this all leads to a kind of instantly blossoming experience of acedia and anhedonia toward the whole thing, just as soon as the notion arises.

And finally, an entry from seven years later, recorded in my journal on Monday, February 24, 2020:

For many years, most of my life, I felt driven to communicate to other people what I was thinking, through the form of the written word. This was partly a matter of intrinsic pleasure and partly a matter of ego gratification.... This egoic motivation was always right there, running equal with the sheer innate desire to articulate, to myself and to others, the thoughts and feelings that burned within me.

So what has happened to change that, to demotivate me on both counts? On the matter of writing fiction, is my lack of productivity these past many years an extended sophomore slump, an interminable round of self-consciousness in which the editor has strangled the creator? Am I letting Resistance win?.... Do I need to... keep writing, keep the flow going, let sheer quantity produce quality as Bradbury recommended, trusting that something good will come through eventually in its own way and on its own schedule? Do I need to trust the very act of writing? Just consider it endless, playful practice with no end result aimed at?

The thing that hamstrings this line of reasoning— which always sounds good whenever I reiterate it — is the sense that arises, after a few days or weeks of this practice, that it's all pointless. Quite simply, I begin to wonder, "Why?" And this is devilishly persuasive, not just the question itself but the state of mind from which it arises. Because it doesn't seem to be resistance as such. Or if it is, then it's damned well camouflaged.

What comes over me is the sense, the thought, that even if I do end up producing a good story or whatever, *so what? What would it even matter?* I mean to me or to anyone else. How could it possibly have any significance? The finished product itself, the time and effort that went into creating it, my experience of writing it, the reactions of the people who would read it, my experience of knowing those responses, the impact the story might have on someone — is there anything really worthwhile in any of that? Isn't there just as much reason not to do it as to do it?

This then bleeds out into the wider question of why to do anything at all.[1]

As you can see, my personal experience of grappling with block, and thus with Resistance, has devolved over time to the question of basic existential motivation — of why to act or not act at all, of why to do or not do anything.

Seeing Through Resistance

More recently, as my understanding of creativity has continued to deepen and evolve, I have begun to discover new levels of subtlety embedded in this negative/enemy pole of the inner creative battle. In a series of entries that I wrote in my journal over several days in the spring of 2021, when I was becalmed at home with my wife during the isolation of the COVID-19 lockdowns — having recently relocated from Texas to Arkansas during the societal shock waves of the pandemic, which left me feeling like I was ensconced in a liminal hyperspace — I rather suddenly realized that a deep understanding of Resistance, including not only how it works but *what it actually is*, down at the base level of the psyche, unravels the riddle of creativity at its ontological root. In the place where the apparently independent self emerges from and merges back into the One Self, the Ground of Being, the Absolute Consciousness, this is where Resistance takes form as an ultimately illusory enemy whose very unreality, when perceived, unlocks the door to creativity on a cosmic scale.

Let me unpack the above claim by describing my personal experience in more granular form. For me, the experience of being conquered in this deep way by Resistance, when I examine it closely, reveals itself as a two-stage or two-layer affair.

In the first stage or layer, as I set out to do some sort of creative work, to enact some nascent idea in tangible form — a story, a song, an essay — I encounter a glitch or barrier consisting of the feeling that either a lack of ideas, or a lack of skill, or the nature of outward circumstances — not enough time, too much stress from my day job, pressure from interpersonal relationships, and so on— is preventing me from carrying out the work. Or sometimes, if I have been in a blocked state for quite some time, I skip past these and run right into the sense of lethargy, futility, and demotivation described above. However it manifests, what happens is that I set out to do something, to do the work, and find that a challenge to my efforts arises immediately, as if by magic. It's as if the challenge is one with the creative impulse itself, a corollary to it, an automatic accompaniment.

So that's the first stage, the top layer: hitting the wall in whatever form. In the second stage, rather than fighting this challenge, I consent to it. This is where, no matter what form the barrier originally took, it morphs into that acquiescent apathy. I embrace an attitude of surrender toward the whole thing, a kind of capitulatory quietism. First I feel the Resistance, along with the suffering of it, the emotional stunting and the crushing sense of frustration and grief. Then I willingly embrace it. I accept the silence, the inability, the paralysis, the muteness. The fight seems hard and the reward of "winning" it seems meaningless, so I sink willingly into inertia.

And so, nothing happens. It has all been an inner drama with no outer result. Anybody watching with physical eyes alone would have seen nothing going on at all, no outward sign of an inner struggle or aborted project. But someone endowed with spiritual sight would have witnessed a slow death taking place.

As you may have noticed, though all of the above represents a detailed inner account, it actually begs a question. This comes into focus when I seek to fathom the mystery of what's really happening, and I find myself returning to the apparently automatic, complementary nature of Resistance. As I said, it is always right there, as if by magic. This is sufficient cause for suspicion.

The fact that Resistance arises simultaneously with the act, or even the intent, of starting to do the work is highly suggestive. On reflection, it seems to imply that something about the way I have positioned myself to work, or maybe the attitude that I bring to it, involves a hidden contradiction. Because truly, why should the effort and intent to do creative work generate its own opposition? Am I missing something? Is something amiss? Could there be something wrong, on some level, with my intent itself?

Light comes from zeroing in on the act of surrender, the moment of giving in to the obstructing force. At that moment the energy from both directions, the creative impulse and the Resistance that opposes it, is discharged in a kind of culmination, however unhappy. The question is: What appears in the brief flash and its aftermath?

I said above that Resistance wins because I willingly embrace it and surrender to it. But now, as I closely observe the moment when this outcome manifests, I find the matter isn't quite as settled as it first appeared. Do I really embrace defeat? How truly willing is my surrender? Do I fully assent to the state of being becalmed, silent, and totally "unproductive" as the impetus to create passes away unfulfilled? Or do I instead wallow and simmer on some level in grief and self-recrimination? Am I actually surrendering, which means giving up entirely and thus letting go of the stress, grief, and unhappiness? Or am I just *capitulating*, which means I give up the fight but still hold on to an inner morass of resentment and grief?

The answer, of course, is the latter. The very fact that my "surrender" results in a state of apathy and anhedonia shows that it isn't really surrender at all. The apathy arises because the pain is too great. Apathy isn't surrender, it's passive-aggressive scorn. It's a defense mechanism. I wouldn't feel it if I had truly let go.

And now, with this surprising recognition of a self-deception at the core of my supposed surrender, the moment of clarity arrives:

How much of my creative block has been subliminally entwined with this self-destructive cast of mind from the start? How much is the experience of silence and quietude as suffering just an unmasking of what was already there, a revealing of the programmed thought-emotion that gave rise to, or first emerged in the guise of, the block itself?

Answer: all of it.

Unmasking Ego

Follow me here: Resistance, it turns out, is actually a cloaked form of an egoic and therefore artificial desire to create. In other words, an egoic counterfeit, as all things egoic always are. The ego thinks "I must create," and being ego, it wants to do this for narcissistic reasons, to shore up its fear-based sense of identity. It wants the self-gratifying and self-enclosed sense of regarding itself, and of having other egos regard it, as creative, brilliant, awesome. So it sets out to write something, to create something, under its own effortful power, for its own narcissistic ends.

But this necessarily engenders Resistance, which is also egoic. Even if we picture Resistance as a truly separate, autonomous force in the cosmos, a true Demonic Angel, it is really, functionally, just the figurehead or archetype of each individual's personal, private experience of it. Resistance with the capital "R," Resistance at large in the universe, is the spiritual nexus and absolute exemplar of the small "r" egoic resistance that we each know as our individual selves, the inflexibility of (seeming) separate, autonomous existence within a world of otherness. Ego is like a resistant screen in the river of consciousness, a net or filter through which pure consciousness flows and into which pure consciousness coalesces. It is, in a real sense, a kind of feedback loop. Identifying with it, as almost everyone does, means identifying with a dream of individual identity, a "me plus (or rather me against) the world" outlook.

This inherent, intrinsic, constitutional egoic resistance is inseparable from the Demonic Angel of creative Resistance. They are one and the same.

The demonic angel archetype of big "R" Resistance is the Ur-ego, the supreme image of self-enclosed, self-seeking self-fulness.

So, a momentous discovery has just announced itself regarding the nature of the block that we encounter in creative work: Resistance is the source of both the artificial desire to create and the accompanying sense of desperate inability to do so.

This leads to the jarring realization that my personal portion of it is, ultimately, a sucker's game. It's a deception, a con. It shows me something with one hand and then hides it with the other. It misdirects as it plays multiple parts and dazzles me with a manipulation of my thoughts and attention. And it's all in a circle, all for the purpose of feeding on my emotional suffering as it reproduces itself in me, in an attempt to alleviate or escape its own suffering by fulfilling its own unfulfillable — because ultimately false — being.

The Magic of Authentic Surrender

This is why, in addition to the various active responses to Resistance that focus on mounting a creative counterattack, and that Pressfield describes so helpfully in *The War of Art*, there is another approach we can take that will undercut the whole thing: authentic passivity. On this count, some penetrating words from

Eckhart Tolle on the matter of stillness and inactivity apply as much here as they do to his focal subject of spiritual awakening:

> [I]s there something you "should" be doing but are not doing it? Get up and do it now. Alternatively, completely accept your inactivity, laziness, or passivity at this moment, if that is your choice. Go into it fully. Enjoy it. Be as lazy or inactive as you can. If you go into it fully and con-sciously, you will soon come out of it. Or maybe you won't. Either way, there is no inner conflict, no resistance, no negativity.[2]

What Tolle describes here is *real* passivity and inactivity, fully em-braced, in contrast to the false, frustrated inactivity of feeling blocked. In authentic surrender, you let go of the notion that you should be doing something.

This short-circuits the Resistance loop, the Resistance con, wherein that Demonic Angel gives with one hand while taking away with the other. Now you are confounding Resistance because you are doing something it can never do and never understand: You're being real. You have stepped off the Resistance ride, and thereby the egoic ride as well, and are freely and authentically Doing Nothing.

The outcome of such an act — or rather non-act — is funda-mentally unpredictable, precisely because you are being truly free instead of acting out a mental-emotional program. Before, you were a robot. Now, you're a person. This distinction is crucial be-cause it highlights the importance of *motivation* in reaching this state. You can't reach it if you seek it for the purpose of escaping Resistance and becoming productive. That merely smuggles the ego in through the back door. To enter this authentic rest, you must truly give up all notion of trying to bring about some predetermined and pre-desired result.

Think again of Tolle's words, and especially the penultimate quoted sentence above: He says that if you go into inactivity "fully and consciously, you will soon come out of it. *Or maybe you won't.*" This little four-word sentence has continued to resonate in my mind and revisit me frequently on long days and dark nights ever since I first read it in 1999. When you truly surrender to inactivity, activity might eventually return — or it might not. If you really want to see your way through Resistance, you have to find a place within yourself, an authentically open-minded and open-hearted position, from which you can honestly say that if activity never returns, you're okay with that. It's fine. You have given up trying to dictate the outcome and judge the results. "Sometimes when we give up and let go, everything's over," says poet and writing teacher Susan Wooldridge. "Other times, our work might just need time to incubate. I can't know whether I've dropped a project or it's just incubating. I think often, we have to let go fully... and accept not knowing."[3]

It is here that creativity, the real kind instead of the ego's attempts to ape it, links most pointedly to the deep nature of not only personal but cosmic reality as a whole. Consider: Why is there anything at all? Why does the experience of self and world, mind and cosmos, the whole play and panoply of Shakespeare's "sound and fury," exist to begin with? What is the source and reason for the ten thousand things, the dream of the world, the created cosmic order? What gives rise to galaxies, nebulae, stars, planets, life, and the screen or page on which a nominally separate "you" is now reading these words? What is the original and present impetus for all things to exist and be as they are?

Embracing the total inactivity of full surrender reconnects you to this original motivation, whatever it is and however we may try to capture it in words: the matrix of creation, the source of all native motive power, God, the Tao. Surrender to stillness creates an "all bets are off" situation in which the question of if, when, and what you will create, of whether and how you will take action at all, is unanswerable, or rather is only answerable in the actual moment of action (or inaction) and creation (or no creation). Action/creation becomes the pure expression of Being itself, seeking either no end at all or — to say functionally the same thing from the human viewpoint — an end that only It knows. If and when you act, you do so simply *to* act, for motives that are pure because they are not your own.

Or rather, these motives are more deeply your own than any you have ever known before, because they emanate from a level of primordial psychological and ontological intimacy that transcends anything you have previously thought of or even suspected as "yourself."

Subplots of Being

Here is a metaphor that we might find useful for illustrating all of this. It's also one that returns us to the very first metaphor and notion that we began with in Chapter One: To align and flow with your innate creativity, learn to recognize your very existence as a story. A narrative created by the universe. A tale being told within Being itself. What you call "your life" is not a mere sequence of events. Rather, it's a story with you as the central character. However, dive deeper and you find it's a fiction. You are a dream character being spun from pure thought within absolute awareness. Only the faculty of memory holds it all together.

John Wheeler offers a clear and helpful account of what's happening here:

> It is all castles in the air being constructed in thought. In a moment, we are conceiving of a past time, a past world, a past entity that was in that kind of world, a memory to hold all that and ourselves as some kind of being present in the middle of it all.

And though the impression that our memories belong or add up to a real "us" is so very vivid, careful introspection reveals what's really going on:

> In present awareness, present thoughts are appearing and disappearing. It is all purely conceptual, purely imagined. Time, the external world and the separate entity are all posited in thought. They are taken as real, but are not actually present as substantial things in themselves.[4]

The situation is very much analogous to what we experience in a dream, where we interact with people and places, and where, as Wheeler puts it, "appropriate memories appear to corroborate everything." But when we wake up later, we see that it was all a mental fabrication, just "appearances taken as real." Moreover, "awareness stands beyond, free and untouched. It is not even in the dream. The dream is in it." And then the transformative point: "It is the same with our present awareness in this apparent waking state.[5]

For some people, especially those who are not accustomed to the nondual style of discourse, assertions like these can feel almost freakishly outré, like outlandish delusions. But that's just a matter of what you're used to hearing, of your relative familiarity, or lack of it, with a certain mode of thinking and talking about life, self, and reality. Forget the verbiage, and just pause to look for yourself: What is really real in your present experience, within the inescapable cradle of your first-personhood, which is categorically all you have ever known or can ever know? Dwell on this and become ruthlessly aware of when you are abstracting away into realms of theorizing and mental chatter based on baseless presuppositions instead of actually attending to what presents itself. The result might be a revelation.

To return to the metaphor and reassert the bridge to writing and art: In your very essence as this separate identity, you are a story. And within this story of you, your creative endeavors are subplots, microcosmic effusions of the prior creative effusion that is their author.

Recognizing this layered symmetry, this descending ontological scale of creation, is the key not only to unlocking your writing but to waking up. It is the convergence point of spiritual awakening and creative production and flow. The more you understand your own story — both the narrative itself (which deserves attention in its own right; you can read your life like a novel) and the truth that it's a story being spun from thought within your absolute identity as pure being-awareness — the more free and profound your writing and art can become, because now their relative place within your overall life experience is clear.

Fundamental issues that can hinder you are now resolved. The dilemma of quietism and demotivation as a conflict with the creative drive is now rendered meaningless. How and why do you — or should you, or can you — write or create? Is there a reason for it? And what about the times when you feel blocked, when Resistance rears its ugly head? These questions are moot. Creation is already happening in the very fact of your existence as this dream character. A story is already being told in the form of you. Now just loop into it with your pen by giving voice to whatever subplots want to emerge: whatever stories, novels, poems, articles, essays, memoirs, screenplays, journal entries, or scratchings in the snow are now suggesting themselves for your devotion and attention, for your presence and participation as their point of entry into this world.

In other words, you are now free to realize your real identity — not through effort or wishful thinking, but through simple, clear, honest, accurate recognition — as an axis of creation. And you are free to enjoy it.

NOTES

1. Cardin, *Journals*, Volume 2, 131, 231–232, 261–262.
2. Eckhart Tolle, *The Power of Now: A Guide to Spiritual Enlightenment* (New World Library, 1999), 69.
3. Susan G. Wooldridge, *Foolsgold: Making Something from Nothing and Freeing Your Creative Process* (Harmony Books, 2007), 77.
4. John Wheeler, *You Were Never Born* (Salisbury, UK: Non-Duality Press, 2013), *https://johnwheelernonduality.wordpress.com/wp-content/Uploads/2020/09/you-were-never-born-john-wheeler-updated.pdf*,26.
5. Ibid., 27.

15

The Teleology of Now

I N THIS penultimate chapter, I build on momentum from the revelation uncovered in the previous one by expanding its argument to encompass life at large and all manner of action in the world, with writing and creativity framed in this larger context. I point this out simply to assure you in advance that as you read what follows, the thread laid down by the previous two chapters and this book as a whole is not lost. It simply enters new territory and gains wider, in fact infinite, scope.

The Acorn and the Oak

We left off with the liberating insight and experience of authentic action undertaken from authentic motivation when we live in aware alignment with the creative current that gives rise to the cosmos. That is the ideal we're maintaining here: a harmonious living relationship with the natural "plan" for each of our lives, as embodied in the figure of the daemon muse, which mediates between the infinite and our concrete finitude. But the question of practicality now raises its head: What does such action *look like*? Concretely, right here and now, what form does such action take?

How does it emerge? How can we know if it is active and unfolding in our life and experience at this very moment?

Assuming that I am in the pocket of the moment as I pose the question — instead of the question itself being a case of my abstracting away from the moment into egoic flights of distraction and delusion, which is quite possible — authentic action for me, for Matt, at this particular moment looks like and takes the form of, well, asking this question.[1] And of reflecting on the asking of it, as I'm doing right now. And of writing these words about it with you in mind. Every moment, which means always *this moment*, becomes its own motivation and fulfillment. Though I may have "goals" that I pursue with a view to "gaining" or "achieving" something, these always have scare quotes around them. They are always secondary and provisional. What is primary and actual is the enduring present moment and the native motivation that ever-emerges within it.

This question of goals, of gaining and achieving, warrants some extended reflection. Intellectual criticism of the recommendation to live purely in and for the moment says this approach encourages and enables capriciousness, flightiness, an inability to retain focus long enough to accomplish anything that requires sustained attention and effort. Such criticism says you will never accomplish anything of value if you don't deliberately commit to long-term goals, an act that — so the criticism goes — fundamentally clashes with abiding in the moment. There are several things to note about this.

First, what guarantees the desirability of goals established and chosen through a focus on the future? Where do such goals come from? What motivates the choosing of them? They are just as likely as not to be products of the Resistance con or ruse, for reasons already articulated.

Second, do the trees and grass and birds outside the windows of my office as I write these words have a future purpose? Do they plan for tomorrow? Aren't they just being and doing what they naturally, natively are and do?[2] The oak tree outside with my bird feeder hanging from its branch — it came from an acorn. Did that acorn employ conscious, deliberate, intellectual thought to become the tree? Sure, the program, the impetus for it to become a tree, was embedded in it as a kind of "goal" — but the acorn didn't think about it. Rather, it just enacted it, manifested it, in spontaneous synergy with the coterminous realities of soil, weather, climate, season, and total environment. The acorn "acted out" its goal in the present moment, patiently, without effort or anxiety, simply doing what it did. Becoming the tree was, so to speak, an afterthought. The inbuilt program was always there, but the specific means of enacting it were always here and now, undertaken spontaneously in and for the moment. The acorn didn't plan or try to become the oak, it just did it, as a teleological imperative in which the telos was always present. And that telos is *still present right now*, still playing out, unfolding, and fulfilling itself even as I look at this lovely tree through the window.

Third, is the oak, or was the acorn, capricious or flighty because it "took no thought for the morrow"? Was it, or is it now, unable to "focus" long enough to "accomplish" anything of value, any real result? Or was and is it the case that its very inhabiting of the eternal present, and its "practice" of living and acting both in and for this moment, is the very source of its stability? The answer to the question of what authentic living looks like is answered here, in the sight and phenomenon of this tree, and in any other like it.

To make clear the connection this is all leading toward: Cannot I, myself, grow with the same stability toward my own worthwhile "goals" — still with scare quotes around them — in the very same way and via the same sustained inhabiting of this moment? Will not my own goals and outcomes be more real, more enduring, less artificial, less subject to self-caused suffering, if I take my motivation always in, from, and for this moment? Am I not playing out the scripted programs of a karmic robot every time I do otherwise, every time I mentally depart from now and begin to seek something in some other imagined moment? I refer not just to the act of mentally envisioning potential actions, outcomes, environments, and scenarios, which is a human capacity to be rightly used, but the mistake, the delusion, of imagining other times and places and *forgetting they are mental projections instead of reality*, and then taking for the ground of my motivation these artificial, mental, synthetic worlds.

Real power, stability, and value of action and outcome always arise from and reside within a focused, patient, dedicated, peaceful state of resting in the present. The complete and authentic goal of anything at all, including my very being-as-Matt and your very being- as-you — the fulfillment of our respective purposes at large — is always found now. Right now is what your authentic life looks like. Right now is when, where, and how your purpose appears, emerges, manifests.

As Alan Watts was fond of saying: This is it. The specific shapes and configurations that arise over time — and again, always now — will do so naturally and will be exactly what they are supposed to be, if and as we express ourselves authentically in this moment, doing (or not doing) what comes to us and from us to do (or not do), making a long-term pattern like Ray Bradbury's narrative tracks spontaneously left in the snow by characters living out their destinies in the present, with each step taken for its own sake alone on a journey of living perpetually into the dark.

Even more: We are living our purpose and seeing it fulfilled even when we don't feel aligned with this moment, when we feel jaggedly crossways with it, out of sync, trapped in apathy, misery, or dysfunction. Such negativity is simply a mental perspective, and is therefore nothing but virtual, a vapor, our own private, personal Matrix. We are free to wake up from it and step out of it at any point. When we do, we find that no ground has been lost. In fact, there was never any to lose.

The Inner Compass

Speaking of feelings, it is useful to consider these things not just from the outside, from the angle of what living in the mode of authentic, spontaneous action looks like, but from the inside, from the angle of what it feels like. When we consciously observe our own experience, this further enriches the answer to our question in Part Two about the potential tension or conflict between creative action and the silence and stillness of spiritual awakening.

To do this, we can give deliberate attention to the respective feelings of egoic motivation and what I will call authentic motivation, which could just as easily be called holistic or divine motivation. This helps us to recognize in an immediate, first-person way how to act — and how to rest — from the vantage point of truth itself. It helps us recalibrate our sense of things by reminding us of what it feels like to lapse unwittingly into an egoic counterfeit of our real self, a pseudo-self that seeks the faux freedom of self-determination in pursuit of selfish and self-serving ends. In other words, it serves as an inner compass.

I will phrase the calibration in first-person singular terms. What I find when I observe myself carefully, noticing my different states and feelings at various times when I realize that I have either become unconsciously identified with the currents of ego or more consciously identified with the wider reality, is this:

- Egoic motivation feels agitated and anxious. Authentic motivation feels relaxed and untroubled.
- Egoic motivation feels heavy and serious. Authentic motivation feels light and playful.
- Ego motivation feels desperate. Authentic motivation feels secure.
- Egoic motivation feels compelled. Authentic motivation feels free.
- Egoic motivation feels restricted. Authentic motivation feels unlimited.
- Egoic motivation feels like grasping, like lack, like incompleteness seeking to gain something that will satisfy or fulfill it. Authentic motivation feels like supply, like satisfaction and fulfillment seeking to express itself.
- Egoic motivation feels pride and shame. It seeks adulation on

the one hand and concealment of its faults and its fundamental sense of inadequacy on the other. Authentic motivation feels a quiet, unprideful, unassailable self-assurance.

- Egoic motivation is hypersensitive and liable to frustration, anger, and irritation. Authentic motivation is mild-mannered, composed, and unperturbed.
- Egoic motivation feels lonely and isolated, "me against the world." Authentic motivation feels connected, harmonious, in flow with things.
- Egoic motivation feels ultimately futile, a search for a satisfaction that I know is only partial, temporary, and unreal. Authentic motivation feels worthwhile, the expression of a wholeness and satisfaction that is complete, sufficient, and meaningful at each step.

In sum, I find that literally every time I feel a sense of demotivation — depression, discouragement, disillusionment, world weariness, any feeling at all on the spectrum of unhappiness, negativity, uselessness, futility, entrapment, or despair — this is produced by a disjunction or disharmony between my ego and my existential or real self. Or more accurately, it is a function or symptom of identifying with my ego instead of with who and what I really am.

I am free to correct this misidentification at any moment. It takes literally no time, effort, or movement. It is an instantaneous shift in perspective that is always available.

The Mirage of Ego

The feeling of futility when we act from the ego is a useful sign or signal because it alerts us to our current state of identification and reminds us of an important truth: The ego itself is, indeed, futility. It is a trap. It is useless, purposeless, a great, meaningless dead end, all sound and fury, signifying nothing. Or rather, it is this *on its own, in its own right.* The ego has no real purpose in itself, no meaning or end in isolation. Instead, its meaning comes from and inheres in the vital processes, the existential self, the wider and deeper matrix of Being out of which it arises.

When the ego is cut off from the inherent meaningfulness of Being, it's like a puppet trying to feel and define its purpose apart from the puppeteer. It's a bit of spray trying to define and feel its nature apart from the ocean. It feels and perceives a lack of meaning because it truly is meaningless by itself. The sense of this, the mental/emotional perception, is accurate. And/but it is felt at first as a profound negativity, a source of anguish, anxiety, deep insecurity, and eventually nihilistic despair. This is even so with avowed egoists who exult in the supposed freedom of egoic self-definition and self-determination, and who exalt the sense of putative egoic autonomy. Such an attitude is merely the ultimate iteration of the ego's combination of self-seeking and self-justification, which inevitably ends in a crash.

However, to put it all this way is to attribute too much power and even reality to the ego unless the ego's dirty little secret is recognized. The secret is this: The whole thing, everything just described, is *only possible because of not-ego.* In parallel with the hoax of Resistance, the ego's very existence is contingent upon something not itself, something beyond and other than itself. Ego is a product of Being's beingness, specifically of Being's ability or capacity to engage in feedback loops that emerge as the relatively real loci of separate consciousness that we perceive and refer to as individual beings or selves. Ego's beingness, in other words, is Being, and this means its meaning is beyond itself. Its origin, nature, and purpose cannot be found in itself. This is not a "problem" until Consciousness becomes conscious as ego and begins to *seek itself* as ego. From that perspective — the perspective of the ego seeking its own significance, and also the significance of the world in which it finds itself, from the vantage point of its own projected sense of separation and autonomy — there appears to be no given meaning, no inherent value or purpose to anything. An ego that seeks and regards itself as its own end has no end. At some point, to some degree, on some level, it will recognize this, either emotionally or intellectually, and usually both.

Egos associated with particularly vibrant centers of individuated selfhood, those with highly developed emotional and cognitive capacities, will feel this meaninglessness all the more vividly, with the greatest power and poignancy. They will write poetry about it, compose music about it, paint pictures to capture and convey the feeling of it, and construct philosophies to articulate it to exquisite levels of sophistication. They will view life as a grand tragedy in which individuals are condemned to hold transcendent aspirations in a universe devoid of transcendent meaning.

What they will not do is see — unless they see through these things by seeing through their very selves — that this is all a kind of cosmic masturbatory fantasy. At no point is Being actually separate from ego, and therefore at no point is ego actually a trap of meaninglessness or futility. Nor is the vision of all reality itself as that meaningless idiot's tale ever true except in the mind of the ego that conceives it. Such a vision is purely a product of projection. The ego rightly senses its own meaninglessness in and of itself, and it reads this into reality at large.

But reality at large, reality itself, which is Being Itself, is not meaningless. In fact, it is pure and absolute meaning. It is its own meaning, and this expresses "outwardly" in the unfolding of the cosmos on all its levels, in all its details and multitudinous manifestations. The ego, all egos, are part of this expression, this unfolding. It is only the capacity of Being-as-consciousness to identify with each and all of its creations that enables ego to become, and to feel itself as, an island of self in an indifferent and disconnected ocean of a world. The very consciousness of futility and meaninglessness is Consciousness itself, which is Being, which is meaning.

Both sides or aspects of the drama — the ego's subjective sense of being a conscious self trapped in despair in a world it never made, and the complementary perceived phenomenon of the mute and meaningless (or perhaps hostile, depending on your core persuasion) universe as the theater of this unhappy and pointless drama — are representations and manifestations of Being.

So, the way out of the trap is to realize that it is all, so to speak, a hoax or a con, just like self-deceiving ruse of creative Resistance. It only seems real as long as I-as-ego identify with and seek my meaning and fulfillment in I-as-ego. If I broaden and deepen the scope of my identification, suddenly everything appears as — is revealed as — meaningful, including the virtual, hallucinatory world of my egoic self-enclosedness and despair.

This despair and all its associated negative subjective states—ennui, apathy, acedia, unhappiness, insecurity, fear, lack, ignorance, trauma, frustration, unfulfilled and unfulfillable longing — I can now recognize as symptoms, and fruitfully receive and use them as pointers toward and tools for awakening. The slightest sense of negativity in any of its shades or modes is a signal that I am, to some degree, on some level, in some way, presently identifying with this ego and trying to find or effect my ultimate fulfillment there, where it can never be found. I have uncovered another area where I can let go, where I can disidentify from this illusion and delusion, and thus explode it by simply letting it be.

The one clear test or demonstration of the hallucinatory nature of the egoic trap of meaninglessness is this: When I piercingly feel the force and weight of the trap and its panic and grief, on those occasions when it becomes painfully real and clear to me, my heart does not stop beating. My breath does not stop cycling. My thoughts and feelings do not stop arising. I do not suddenly vanish from the earth. My physical being and its environment go right on expressing and embodying the meaning and purpose of Being. The despair is just a mental phenomenon, an abstracted illusion, a thought and associated emotion of an alienation that is only real in and as thought and emotion. It would not even be possible to think and feel it apart from the base reality of Being and therefore meaning.

Creative Quietude

What happens when this realization dawns in our lives? How do our writing, our art, our creativity, and our very selves transform and realign? Two chapters ago, I quoted Jacob Needleman on the state in which we come to "open within ourselves to the great flow of fundamental forces that constitute the ultimate nature of the universe," which enables our behavior to let "the central, creative power of the universe to manifest through it."

Needleman was writing within the context of Taoism, in an introduction that he provided to a modern English translation of the *Tao Te Ching*. The term for this state of effortless action, of being moved not by our personal effort but by alignment with the current of reality itself, is what Taoists have famously called *wu wei*. The term I just used, "effortless action," is probably the most widely known English rendering of this Chinese term. And it is a fairly effective one. But there is another translation that may express the meaning a bit better, and that brings out the main point we have been reaching toward.

Huston Smith, the late scholar of comparative religion, introduced the term in his classic book, *The World's Religions*, in the chapter on Taoism. Smith observes that it's easy to get the wrong idea when it comes to *wu wei*, which is the central point around which the Taoist way of life revolves. Since the term translates literally as "inaction," it can seem to be a counsel of resignation or do nothing-ism. However, the term actually refers to a mode of acting "in which friction — in interpersonal relationships, in intra-psychic conflict, and in relation to nature, is reduced to the minimum."[3] Smith says one possible rendering of this mode is "total effectiveness." Another is "creative quietude." And with this latter term, we have our master key.

"Creative quietude," says Smith, "combines within a single individual two seemingly incompatible conditions — supreme activity and supreme relaxation." He says these are able to coexist in our lives "because human beings are not self-enclosed entities" but rather "ride an unbounded sea of *Tao* that sustains them, as we would say, through their subliminal minds." This leads Smith to reflect on the two minds, the conscious and unconscious. He notes the different modes of activity that are associated with each of these in the creative act. For our purposes here, it is not immaterial to note that his words resound all the way back to the distinction between the two inner voices in the act of writing, the creative and the critical, with which we began our exploration of creativity in the present book. Smith says:

> One way to create is through following the calculated directives of the conscious mind. The results of this mode of action, however, are seldom impressive; they tend to smack more of sorting and arranging than of inspiration. Genuine creation, as every artist knows, comes when the more abundant resources of the subliminal self are somehow tapped. But for this to happen a certain dissociation from the surface self is needed. The conscious mind must relax, stop standing in its own light, let go. Only so is it possible to break through the law of reversed effort in which the more we try the more our efforts boomerang.[4]

Smith goes on to say that in contrast to this blowback effect from conscious, effortful action, *wu wei* or creative quietude "is the supreme action, the precious suppleness, simplicity, and freedom that flows from us, or rather through us, when our private egos and conscious efforts yield to a power not their own." The person who taps into this flow "works without working," displaying extraordinary skill that somehow appears totally natural. "Such a one acts without strain, persuades without argument, is eloquent without flourish, and achieves results without violence, coercion, or pressure."[5]

We don't have to be Taoists to appreciate this vision, nor to incorporate it into our own lives and creative work. Throughout this book, in talking about writing into the dark, and living into the dark, and writing with the daemon muse, and reaching the flashpoint of silence where we realize we are content with total quiet and stillness, and then finding our way past what may feel like a creative and spiritual impasse when we see through Resistance and realize our natural, given identity as an axis of spontaneous creation — throughout all this, the principle of creative quietude has been whispering, including in the deeply personal experiences and states of mind and soul from my life's journey that I have shared with you. The synthesis of effort with relaxation expands our identity and puts us in sync with the creative flow of the cosmos. Conversely, setting effort and relaxation apart and pitting them against each other cuts us off.

Recognizing the truth of this principle, not just abstractly but concretely, in the specific circumstances of your life, and working gently with yourself to actuate it — perhaps, say, by adopting the model of the daemon muse and learning to work with creativity as an intelligent other within you who bears your unique stamp, and with whom you collaborate — expands the flow of your writing in alignment with the metaphysical current that gives rise to self and world. Your ends as a person become Being's very ends. There is no possibility of frustration, despair, ennui, and all the rest, because Being is intrinsically and infinitely meaningful. Your awareness and actions are now infused with that, and they naturally, effortlessly express and fulfill that, just as the circulation of your blood, the growth of your hair and fingernails, and all the processes of your physical body, along with the flowing of water and air currents, the growth and movement of plant and animal life, the workings of meteorological and geological processes, the spinning of this planet, and the motions and cycles of the stars and galaxies, have always been and always are expressions of meaning, of Being, of the intelligence and purpose that shapes and animates all things.

In this marriage of conscious and unconscious, deliberate and spontaneous, action and stillness, sound and silence, self and other, light and dark, we enact our purpose in the sheer fact of existing, including our engagement with whatever specific work comes to us and through us to do. We write and live into the dark, simultaneously blazing and illuminating the path we were born to follow, the famous "pathless path" of Zen. And we find it to be a perfect path, exactly what our hearts desire. In fact, desire and reality are no longer distinguishable from each other. Creative quietude takes us where we both want and need to go in the world and in our lives, because wanting and needing are now inseparable from the undercurrents of reality itself, which shape everything, including us, exactly as we must be.

NOTES

1. Regarding the phrase "pocket of the moment," see Blue Öyster Cult's wonderful song "Pocket," which they released during a period (the early 2000s) when most people thought this iconic band didn't even exist anymore. With lyrics written by horror and science fiction legend John Shirley, who also happens to be a long-time student of and writer on spiritual matters, "Pocket" is a song about waking up in the heart of the now and finding all the vibrancy of life and identity right here, manifesting in the vivid details of whatever arises and presents itself in this eternal present.

2. It wasn't until I went to edit this paragraph and passage after having initially drafted it that I noticed how closely and clearly — and also unconsciously — its central metaphor, and not only that but the very wording of its opening sentence, echoes Emerson's famous words in "Self-Reliance" about the contrast between the vibrant present eternity of nature and the human reluctance or inability to simply be and say what we are. This is a valuable reminder, at least for me, of how often inspiration has a more mundane proximate cause in the fact of influence, aside from — or often in tandem with — infusions from the inner genius. In any case, Emerson's words are always worth remembering and quoting, especially in the current context: "These roses under my window make no reference to former roses or to better ones; they are for what they are; they exist with God to-day. There is no time to them. There is simply the rose; it is perfect in every moment of its existence. Before a leaf-bud has burst, its whole life acts; in the full-blown flower there is no more; in the leafless root there is no less. Its nature is satisfied, and it satisfies nature, in all moments alike."

3. Huston Smith, *The World's Religions* (HarperSanFrancisco, 1991), 200.

4. Ibid., 208.

5. Ibid., 208, 210.

16

Creative Purpose in a Collapsing World

Everyone must leave something behind when he dies....
A child or a book or a painting or a house or a wall built or
a pair of shoes made. Or a garden planted. Something your hand
touched some way so your soul has somewhere to go when you die,
and when people look at that tree or that flower you planted, you're
there.... The most important single thing we had to pound into
ourselves was that we were not important.... We're nothing more
than dust-jackets for books, of no significance otherwise.
— RAY BRADBURY, *Fahrenheit 451*

Your own self-realization is the greatest
service you can render the world.
— RAMANA MAHARSHI

The Path Unveiled: A Retrospective
In many ways, this has been a book of perspectives and metaphors. Though I have offered practical advice here and there, especially in Chapter Four on divining your daemon muse, I have devoted far more space to laying out different angles on and symbolic representations of reality, spiritual awakening, human selfhood, and the creative drive that is embodied in both our specific acts of

artistic creation and our whole lives. Are these helpful? Are they usable or actionable? That is for you to judge. I just know that in my own experience, it has often been not so much the practical advice but the new thought, the fresh perspective, the transformative insight shared by another person, that has been most valuable, sometimes to the point of sparking a wholesale paradigm shift with cascading effects throughout my understanding of myself and my world. Thoreau's famous words in *Walden* about the power of books leaped off the page the first time I read them at age twenty, articulating a truth that still arrests me today:

> There are probably words addressed to our condition exactly, which, if we could really hear and understand, would be more salutary than the morning or the spring to our lives, and possibly put a new aspect on the face of things for us. How many a man has dated a new era in his life from the reading of a book! The book exists for us, perchance, which will explain our miracles and reveal new ones.

A number of books have come to me in the course of my life that have had the effect Thoreau describes. Each has opened a new era for me by catalyzing a paradigm shift. I suppose the importance of this effect in my life has lurked behind my intuitive approach to writing this book, resulting in something that is as much or more about suggesting a shift in your own paradigm as it is about offering applied techniques for enhancing your writing or other creative work.

One of the first metaphors I introduced was that of darkness,

and of writing and living into the dark. As I said in the introduction, the writing of this book has been an implementation and
illustration of that very approach. We then began Part One with multiple meditations on writing and collaborating with the daemon
muse. In Part Two we moved on to consider various angles on the
rich and sometimes subjectively fraught and tense interplay between spirituality, silence, and the drive to write and create. In Part
Three we have examined and exposed Resistance, uncovering a
revelation about its devious nature, and discovering the alignment
with the creative energy of the cosmos that is ours when we see
through the lies of that ultimately illusory enemy.

Here in this concluding chapter, as I continue to follow the
same thread into the darkness of the unplanned and the unknown,
I want to offer yet another perspective by saying something about
locating our creative work within what is commonly referred to as
"the real world," meaning the world of human society and culture.

One of my core fascinations, which I know you share, centers
on the idea of finding and fulfilling our individual "great work,"
whether in the esoteric/occult sense that I mentioned in Chapter
Four or the sense that Stephen Cope, the author, psychologist, and
Kripalu Yoga teacher, employs in his excellent book, *The Great
Work of Your Life*. Cope describes a person's great work as an individual dharma or calling that is lived out on the ground, so to speak,
within and through the vicissitudes and circumstances of a real human life. "People actually feel happiest and most fulfilled," says Cope,

> when meeting the challenge of their dharma *in the
> world*, when bringing highly concentrated effort to some

compelling activity for which they have a true calling.... At the end of life, most of us will find that we have felt most filled up by the challenges and successful struggles for mastery, creativity, and full expression of our dharma in the world. Fulfillment happens not in *retreat* from the world but in *advance* — and profound engagement.[1]

Cope links this point to the famous saying in the Gospel of Thomas that if you bring forth what is inside you, it will save you, but if you don't, it will destroy you. Anyone who has had the experience of living for years in a state of creative block, paralyzed by the spell and swindle of Resistance, compensating for not doing his real work by doing other things that may be nominally worthy, but that ultimately represent a deflection and retreat from what he knows he is really here to do — in other words, anyone like me (and maybe you?) — can personally attest to the truth of this ancient warning.

With all that, what I'm winding my way toward saying is this: Authentic life purpose that is aligned with reality and embodied in one's authentic great work can serve as what we may call a *monastic option.* By this, I don't mean solely the choice, which I mentioned in Chapter One, to make your life a portable monastery of the muse, though that is included. What I mean in a broader sense is what the cultural historian and social critic Morris Berman meant when, inspired in a contemporary American context by the actions of the famous fourth-century Catholic Irish monks who "saved civilization," he coined or reappropriated the term "monastic option" to refer to opting out of the frantic worldview and lifestyle of American and Americanized consumer-capitalist culture so that you can devote yourself to preserving some precious and humane form of knowledge or way of living in the midst of a rising dark age.

This is something I alluded to obliquely in the introduction when I mentioned the value of learning to commune and collaborate with one's daemon muse in an apocalyptic world situation. To repeat what I said there, and to combine it with Chapter Three's exploration of the "daemon in exile": As the world grows weirder and more disturbed, leading toward a potential collective cataclysm, the discipline of the daemon muse may enable us to heal the fateful historical-cultural-psychic rupture that has led us to deny and exclude the visionary aspect of our being from our mainstream map of reality. This heedless act of dissociation rendered our daemon-self destructive in the mold and mode of the Frankenstein myth, where Victor's monster is actually the embodiment of his own rejected daemon, now helplessly transformed into a demonic fury seeking to reconnect with its creator through violence. Reconnecting with this inner force through healthier and more intelligent means may enable us both to resolve this inner-outer crisis and to find a life of meaning and purpose by fulfilling our unique callings right in the midst of a new dark age. It may also enable us to help others not only now but in the world ahead by planting cultural seeds that will come to fruition on the other side of the apocalypse, in a future renaissance.

I mentioned that I would say more about this at the end of the book. That moment has now arrived.

Creativity as a Monastic Option in a Collapsing Culture

Sociocultural issues, as you know, have not been our main concern in this book. But they are certainly not divorced from it either. All creative work, along with all living and spiritual seeking, occurs within some concrete context. Understanding how this context shapes us, and how we reciprocally shape it, is a matter of no small importance. For me, Berman's concept of the monastic option has provided a meaningful model to understand and act on this within the world circumstance of unfolding apocalypse in our current age.

Berman introduced the monastic option in his 2000 book *The Twilight of American Culture*. The book lays out a fundamental diagnosis and critique, both academic and polemical, of America at the dawn of the twenty-first century. Berman characterizes the United States as a country and culture that is past its peak and on the downhill slope of collapse, having fallen into the same sorts of degenerative troubles — social, cultural, economic, political — that have afflicted late-stage empires throughout history. Importantly, he says his point is not to solve the problem. Rather, it is to argue, using a combination of scholarly analysis and personal impressions, that America as a culture, a nation, and a world power has entered its twilight phase and is inevitably headed nowhere but down. He also argues, again referencing the witness of history, that this is a situation where most efforts to address the decline are actually symptoms and functions of it, and thus only serve recursively, and unwittingly, to advance it.

As an American and a human, I find Berman's book to be deeply bracing and stirring. Perhaps the most stirring part, to me, is his concept of the monastic option. Berman suggests that in the face of this irreversible cultural breakdown, which is likely to spool out into the indefinite future, one of the most spiritually and practically beneficial things an individual can do is to follow the example of those Irish monks by finding some worthwhile area of endeavor — a field of knowledge, a set of skills, a plan for a humane way of living, whatever calls deeply to you — and deliberately seeking a way to preserve and transmit it to whatever new culture will arise in the future, after the present one has burned itself to the ground.

To illustrate the point, Berman explicitly points not just to history, and not just to what he takes to be new monastic efforts (his specific examples being those that were underway in America at the turn of the millennium), but to various manifestations of this theme in apocalyptic and dystopian science fiction. He considers, for example, Ray Bradbury's *Fahrenheit 451* — still one of the most prescient among the classic dystopian novels — and its "book people," as they were called in director François Truffaut's 1966 film adaptation, who memorize and effectively become books in an age when reading is banned. They thus preserve books in a line of oral transmission so that one day, when societal conditions have changed, their knowledge can be written down again.

It is Berman's specific characterization of the necessarily private and individual nature of the monastic option, and of the need for all such efforts to retain their countercultural status in order to avoid being corrupted by the very world they are seeking to overcome, that resonates most intensely with me. Every time I revisit his words, I feel the same surge of electric energy, the same rising current of affirmation, that I felt when I first read them two decades ago. I will quote from them at some length because I think they play right into our presiding concern with creativity and life purpose. I am of course writing these words, and you are reading them, within a surrounding societal and cultural circumstance. Things being what they are, I would wager that no matter when it is that we have come together like this in these pages, no matter what year it is or where you specifically happen to be in the world, the global situation, and probably your more immediately local one as well, is both troubled and troubling in some pertinent way. Which means Berman's words, too, remain pertinent:

> An important aspect of the new monastic option is... a rejection... of the group, and of attempts at institutional-ization. Today's "monk" is committed to a *renewed* sense of self, and to the avoidance of groupthink. The monastic option will not be served by the new monastic "class" be-ing a class of any sort.... [T]he power of this contribution lies precisely in its *lack* of institutionalization....
>
> The more individual the activity is, and the more out of the public eye, the more effective it is likely to be in the long run. Not that like-minded souls shouldn't make connections, but the key is to keep the links informal....
>
> [T]hose genuinely committed to the monastic option need to stay out of the public eye; to do their work quiet-ly and deliberately avoid media attention. Indeed, a Tao-ist rule of thumb might be that if the larger culture knows about it, then it's not the real thing....

The job of preservation and transmission at the present time... consists in creating "zones of intelligence" in a private, local way, and then deliberately keeping them out of the public eye.[2]

Berman goes on to suggest three categories or fronts where the monastic option might be carried out. They are specific to America and the parts of the world that fall under its cultural influence, so local modifications or alternatives might be needed. But since the scope of America's influence is global, with every part of the world being affected in some way, there is an aspect of universality to these points. There is also the additional fact that, in a real sense, every culture and civilization, as well as each human life, represents a sustained unfolding of apocalypse, with the truth first concealing itself in the specific forms that compose an individual or collective identity, and then corrosively unmaking them when, through the course of unfolding evolution, this structure departs from its source principle and elaborates itself into a faulty superstructure that must inevitably collapse, like the house built on sand that Jesus talked about.

One of Berman's monastic fronts lies in efforts to expose the emptiness of the consumer-capitalist way of life. A second is to pursue alternative modes of education for developing and preserving intelligence and spirit. A third is environmental design, "work that improves the health of society by altering the mental and visual landscape that we all move in."[3] I expect that you, like me, can easily see how each of these could intersect directly with writing and any other creative and artistic pursuits to which we feel called.

But even so, I would like to suggest a fourth front, and one that tilts the matter in a different direction: that of creativity, clarification of purpose, and spiritual awakening for their own sakes. Both singly and in combination, these are strategies for cultivating health, wholeness, and sane perspective in an insane world — not just for individuals, not merely as a private, self-centered concern with your own development and happiness, but for others, for everyone, for the whole world. And they are applicable regardless of the time or place in which you live.

The Monastery of Your Life

To switch tracks, metaphors, and books under discussion: At one point in 2005's *A New Earth* — whose unifying theme, as stated in the subtitle, is "awakening to your life's purpose" — Eckhart Tolle considers the different kinds of spiritually and creatively awakened activity that can be taken in the world, and also the different modes of living and acting that different people will be natively drawn to by their internal compass and temperament. Some of these modes are active, taking the form of building things and completing projects, as fueled by inspiration and enthusiasm.

But Tolle also identifies a category of people whom he terms "frequency holders." These are individuals with a contemplative streak who don't feel motivated to get deeply involved in the world or work to change it. Their calling is instead to bring stillness and harmony through the simple act of maintaining conscious presence. "They are here," says Tolle, "to generate consciousness through the activities of daily life, through their interactions with others as well as through 'just being.'" He emphasizes the critical importance of this role in a frenetic society that is intent on trying to escape from itself, and that is wreaking much havoc in the process — a society, I note, much like Berman's characterization of twilight-stage America. "In ages past," Tolle says,

> they would probably have been called contemplatives. There is no place for them, it seems, in our contemporary civilization. On the arising new earth, however, their role is just as vital as that of the creators, the doers, the reformers. Their function is to anchor the frequency of the new consciousness on this planet.[4]

I have thrown a lot of different ideas out there in these final pages, so let me draw the various strands together: What I have in mind when I describe all these things and relate them to our guiding concern with creativity, life purpose, nonduality, and the daemon muse is a fusion of Tolle's frequency holders with Berman's New Monastic Individual, carried out within a creative-artistic context. The result is a person who is guided and grounded from within by a living relationship with their creative source, whether we call it the daemon muse or any other appropriate name, of which there are many.

Moreover, such a person is guided by a conscious understanding that this source, which is their inner compass and the spiritual bearer and emblem of the true self, the perfect will, the Great Work their life, opens out more widely in the end, and in fact shades through imperceptible gradations of expanding identity into the Infinite and Absolute. From this position, the person not only finds meaning but *is* meaning. An individual like this channels meaning into a world that desperately needs it, simply by living in alignment with Being.

"[Y]ou can choose a way of life that becomes its own 'monastery,' preserves the treasures of our heritage for yourself, and, hopefully, for future generations," says Berman.[5] In the model I am proposing, these "treasures" refer not only to the objects, knowledge, and ways of being that a specific culture and civilization has produced, but to our Original Being, the spiritual source of what we are and what the world is. This monastery of one's life is where a living connection with reality — I want to give it a capitalization for divine emphasis: Reality — is maintained, and again, not for purely private enjoyment or benefit, but for the leavening and healing influence that this inevitably and inexorably, and also quietly and subtly, broadcasts to others.

Berman quotes Don DeLillo on the idea that being marginal in a culture like twilight-stage America is likely to make a writer not less significant but more so: "In the end, writers will write not to be outlaw heroes of some underculture but mainly to save themselves, to survive as individuals."[6] I can't help but think of this in connection with the famous lines from Ramana Maharshi about the relationship between saving oneself and saving the world:

The sage helps the world merely by being the real Self.[7]

Realisation of the Self is the greatest help that can be rendered to humanity. Therefore, the saints are said to be helpful, though they remain in forests.[8]

Is it folly to think like this about the role of writers and artists as new monks in a collapsing culture? As people who serve in the role of frequency holder? As centers of sanity in a world gone mad? As individuals who choose a way of life that becomes its own monastery by putting them in alignment and living relationship with the creative current of the cosmos through the intermediary of their daemon muse? If this is folly, then consider me a fool.

I am well aware of the other side of the argument, the easy observation of the many ways in which the creative-artistic life can go completely off the rails, tilting over into self-absorption, substance abuse, poverty, poisoned relationships, depression, delusions of grandeur, and a few other personal disasters I could mention. History, and also the present, is littered with real-life examples. But when it's working right, when the excesses and imbalances are corrected or avoided, and when a writer establishes a genuine working relationship of creative quietude in sync with their muse, daimon, daemon, or inner genius, this opens a channel for transcendent meaning to flow into the world. Such meaning sustains both the world and the writer, fulfilling the purpose of each and infusing the journey of writing and living into the dark with a palpable aura of focus, confidence, steadiness, and wisdom that radiates both from the person and from the work.

The specific details, the way this might manifest and look in someone's actual experience — maybe yours, maybe mine — are various. They are also difficult or impossible to predict, since they shift with the leading edge of the moment as embodied in the practical circumstances of a given life, flowing and taking shape like the suppleness of water that Taoism is so fond of pointing to. The step of getting clear about what this might mean in applied terms for your own life and practice as a writer, or an artist or seeker, and for your whole life and creative destiny — the question of what to do, of how to enact this vision if it resonates with you — is specific to the unique phenomenon, the singular wave in the ocean of the world, that is you. It therefore lies beyond my ability to articulate here. What I can do is articulate the vision itself, on the chance that it will indeed resonate, and that it might even serve as those Thoreauvian "words addressed to our condition exactly, which, if we could really hear and understand, would be more salutary than the morning or the spring to our lives, and possibly put a new aspect on the face of things for us."

The Cosmic Slipstream

I close with a final metaphor. It is one that draws together the different strands this book has woven together from the darkness of the unknown, and the practice of living and writing freely into it, and the felt tension between the call to write or create and the spiritual call toward silence and stillness, and the seeing-through of Resistance to uncover an experience of oneness with the creative impulse that animates the cosmos, and the vision of the creative frequency holder as a new monk who makes a monastery of their life to shelter, preserve, and transmit something sacred beyond the rim of the apocalypse, thus fulfilling while also transcending the calling that is made known in the energy and inspiration of the daemon muse.

Alan Watts ended the first chapter of his classic *The Book: On the Taboo against Knowing Who You Are* — which is about seeing through the illusion of being an isolated ego that is separate from the universe — by addressing what some might see as a contradiction in his act of writing such a book at all. On the one hand, he said, his book contains "no sermons, no shoulds and oughts" about awakening. This is because

> on seeing through the illusion of the ego, it is impossible to think of oneself as better than, or superior to, others for having done so. In every direction there is just the one Self playing its myriad games of hide-and-seek. Birds are not better than the eggs from which they have broken. Indeed, it could be said that a bird is one egg's way of becoming other eggs. Egg is ego, and bird is the liberated Self.... [I]t is not impossible that the play of the Self will be to remain unawakened in most of its human disguises.[9]

But on the other hand, Watts was indeed writing a book about seeing through the illusion of the ego. So why, then, was he even writing on such a topic if not in the spirit of an "ought"? Watts confronted the question head-on, and he did so in a way that has wider implications than just the matter of his book, for his words lift the veil on why any of us are doing anything at all. The motive he described for his activity of writing and teaching is actually the real motive behind all the respective appearances of motion and activity in these wave formations that we call our lives and ourselves:

If, then, I am not saying that you ought to awaken from the ego-illusion and help save the world from disaster, why *The Book*? Why not sit back and let things take their course? Simply that *it is part of "things taking their course" that I write.* As a human being it is just my nature to enjoy and share philosophy. I do this in the same way that some birds are eagles and some doves, some flowers lilies and some roses.[10]

If you want to receive it, there is a significant clue here for identifying or clarifying your daemon muse, your Great Work, your unique combination of intrinsic drives, gifts, interests, ideas, and calling — not as a matter of passively or even fatalistically accepting life's events, but as a matter of actively participating in their unfolding, and thereby understanding something about the architecture of the monastery that might be made of your life.

The clue is concealed, openly, in this: Based on the dance or gestalt of motive and manifestation that is active in your experience even now, what does "things taking their course" look like for the singularity, the projected identity of uniqueness, that bears the name on your birth certificate? As you live and write your way into the dark, what is the pathless path that reveals itself one step at a time, manifesting spontaneously in the edge of the moment, even as it also illuminates a journey that was always there before you, just waiting to be taken? How has your whole life up to now, in all its inner and outer details, served as a long-form demonstration and revelation of the answer to that question? When you read your life backwards, what has everything always been leading up to? The answer, of course, is this moment. And what does everything about this moment, with its backstory and present complement of living themes and tendencies, point toward on the path ahead, beyond the edge of the lantern light illuminating the shadows on the course set before you?

What is the precise step you need to take right now, within that golden glow, to advance on the path? What single thing can you do at this moment, listening not to the dominant culture around you but to your own deepest internal guidance, that represents things taking their course?

Watts's *The Book* was first published in 1966. Four years later, the nonduality writer/teacher William Samuel — who bore the impressive pedigree of having been the first American student of Ramana Maharshi — published *The Awareness of Self-Discovery*, a kind of sequel or companion to his earlier *A Guide to Awareness and Tranquillity* (1967). Bearing the subtitle or tagline "How to Live the Real Identity," this second book contains a passage that articulates the same point Watts addressed, and in a similarly frank and winning way.

The passage comes in a reprinted letter that Samuel sent to a correspondent who had written to him with a question about his emphasis on the importance of judgelessness, the attitude of recognizing and then withdrawing our standard but unacknowledged attitude of judging all appearances — everything that arises in our experience — as either good or bad, positive or negative, desirable or undesirable. "It is our attachment to 'value out there' that has us writhing in agony over what an 'out there' appears to do or not do," Samuel says. But this naturally arouses an objection that is pretty much identical to the one Watts faced: Is not the very recommendation to recognize and relinquish our judging an attitude of judgment itself, since it assigns a negative or problematic value to the act of judging? Samuel addresses this implicit question with the following words, which line up perfectly with Watts's point:

> I have spent a lot of time with this letter because — looking on your letter without judgment, without personal evaluation and without feeling that Allness is anything less than perfect — it seems to be right, fitting, proper, and correct (or whatever word one wishes to use to connote tending to one's business as it comes to him to tend) to write you this clarification.[11]

"Tending to one's business as it comes to him to tend." That, my friends, is the heart of the matter, with "the matter" being how to live at the crossroads of creativity and being. Combined with an active embrace of "things taking their course," it provides a wise and practical formulation for how to approach, regard, and receive the entirety of your lived experience, including the outworking of your drive to write and anything and everything else that comes up.

Nisargadatta Maharaj, a contemporary of Ramana Maharshi, put it this way:

> When effort is needed, effort will appear. When effortlessness becomes essential, it will assert itself. You need not push life about. Just flow with it and give yourself to the task of the present moment, which is the dying now to the now.[12]

He also said:

> There is no power as separate from me. It is inherent in my very nature. Call it creativity.... What you call the universe, nature, is my spontaneous creativity. Whatever happens — happens.... To want nothing, to do nothing — that is true creation! To watch the universe emerging and subsiding in one's heart is a wonder.[13]

Once, in spiritual conversation with a seeker, Nisargadatta said something that not only illustrates these principles but aligns per-fectly with Samuel's words to his correspondent: "The same power that makes the fire burn and the water flow, the seeds sprout and the trees grow, makes me answer your questions."[14] This is an attitude that we all could — I do not say should, since that introduces division and false effort — take to heart, let flow, and find much greater happiness and fulfillment in so doing.

And now the final metaphor that I promised:

Your life, your sense of separate individuality and the attendant creative drive that it both contains and represents, is a cosmic slip-stream. It is an existential wake trailing behind the unfolding appearance of the universe, emerging from and within the eternal point of here and now, where the wellspring of Being flows.

Live and write from there.

NOTES

1. Stephen Cope, *The Great Work of Your Life: A Guide for the Journey to Your True Calling* (Bantam Books, 2012), xxiv (Cope's emphases).

2. Morris Berman, *The Twilight of American Culture* (W. W. Norton, 2000), 88–89, 130–131, 134 (Berman's emphases).

3. Ibid., 154.

4. Eckhart Tolle, *A New Earth: Awakening to Your Life's Purpose* (Penguin Books, 2016), 307.

5. Morris Berman, *The Twilight of American Culture*, 157.

6. Quoted in Berman, *The Twilight of American Culture*, 158.

7. Ramana Maharshi, *Be As You Are: The Teachings of Ramana Maharshi*, ed. David Godman (Arkana, 1985), 150.

8. Ramana Maharshi, *Talks with Ramana Maharshi* (Sri Ramanasramam, 2006), 16.

9. Alan Watts, *The Book: On the Taboo against Knowing Who You Are* (Pantheon Books, 1966), 20.

10. Ibid., 21 (my emphasis).

11. William Samuel, *The Awareness of Self-Discovery* (Mountain Brook Publication Company, 1970), 56.

12. Nisargadatta Maharaj, *I Am That*, 140.

13. Ibid., 138, 140.

14. Ibid., 222.

Bibliography

Abell, Arthur M. *Talks with Great Composers*. Carol Publishing Group, 1994.

Angus, Kate, "Maybe the Secret to Writing Is Not Writing?" *Literary Hub*, September 24, 2019. *https://lithub.com/maybe-the-secret-to-writing-is-not-writing*.

Bajani, Andrea. "Love Is Space: Notes on Marriage and Creativity." Translated by Elizabeth Harris. *Literary Hub*, May 2, 2022. *https://lithub.com/love-is-space-notes-on-marriage-and-creativity*.

Berman, Morris. *The Twilight of American Culture*. W. W. Norton, 2000.

Bradbury, Ray. *Bradbury Stories: 100 of His Most Celebrated Tales*. William Morrow, 2003.

———. *Fahrenheit 451*. 60th Anniversary ed. New York: Simon & Schuster, 2013. Originally published 1953.

———. *Zen in the Art of Writing: Releasing the Creative Genius within You*. Bantam, 1992.

Brande, Dorothea. *Becoming a Writer*. TarcherPerigee, 1981. Originally published 1934.

Cardin, Matt. *A Course in Demonic Creativity: A Writer's Guide to the Inner Genius*. 2011.

———. *Journals*, Volume 2: 2002–2022. Sarnath Press, 2023.

———. *What the Daemon Said: Essays on Horror Fiction, Film, and Philosophy*. Hippocampus Press, 2022.

Carse, David. *Perfect Brilliant Stillness: Beyond the Individual Self*. Non-Duality Press, 2005.

Cope, Stephen. *The Great Work of Your Life: A Guide for the Journey to Your True Calling*. Bantam Books, 2012.

Donaldson-Evans, Catherine. "An Interview with Sci-Fi Legend Ray Bradbury." *Fox News*, November 23, 2004. *https://www.foxnews.com/story/an-interview-with-sci-fi-legend-ray-bradbury*.

Emerson, Ralph Waldo. "Self-Reliance." In *Essays and Lectures*, edited by Joel Porte, 259–282. Library of America, 1983.

Fergeson, Bob. *The Listening Attention*. TAT Foundation Press, 2010.

Gardner, John. *On Becoming a Novelist*. W. W. Norton & Company, 1999.

Goldberg, Natalie. *Writing Down the Bones: Freeing the Writer Within*. Shambala: 1986.

Hemingway, Ernest. "Ernest Hemingway — Banquet Speech." Acceptance speech for the 1954 Nobel Prize in Literature. The Nobel Prize. *https://www.nobelprize.org/prizes/literature/1954/hemingway/speech*. Accessed August 7, 2025.

Hillman, James. *The Soul's Code: In Search of Character and Calling*. Warner Books, 1996.

Holiday, Ryan. *The Obstacle Is the Way: The Timeless Art of Turning Trials into Triumph*. Portfolio, 2014.

Jung, C. G. *Memories, Dreams, Reflections*. Revised edition. Edited by Aniela Jaffé. Translated by Richard and Clara Winston. Vintage Books, 1989.

King, Stephen. *On Writing: A Memoir of the Craft*. Scribner, 2020.

Klein, Jean. *I Am*. Compiled and edited by Emma Edwards. Non-Duality Press, 2007.

La Ronn, Michael. "Writing into the Dark: Write a Book Without an Outline!" YouTube, June 22, 2018, 09:47: *https://youtu.be/w33JlZsVJYI?si=hiQU7rtLCeT3srPb*

Ligotti, Thomas. *My Work Is Not Yet Done: Three Tales of Corporate Horror*. Mythos Books, 2002.

Magee, Rosemary M., ed. *Conversations with Flannery O'Connor*. University Press of Mississippi, 1987.

Maitland, Sara. *A Book of Silence*. Counterpoint, 2008.

Marcus Aurelius. *Meditations*. Translated by George Hays. Modern Library, 2002.

——. *Meditations*: The Annotated Edition. Translated and edited by Robin Waterfield. Basic Books, 2021.

Martel, J. F. *Reclaiming Art in the Age of Artifice: A Treatise, Critique, and Call to Action*. Basic Books, 2025.

Maybe Logic: The Lives and Ideas of Robert Anton Wilson. Directed by Lance Bauscher. The Maybe Logic Academy, 2003. YouTube video, 1:25:30. Posted by "Michael Doubet," January 3, 2013. *https://youtu.be/A7N6TOFyrLg*.

Maybe Logic: The Lives and Ideas of Robert Anton Wilson (transcript). Antilogicalism. Last modified May 6, 2016. *https://antilogicalism.com/2016/05/06/maybe-logic*.

Morrell, David. *The Successful Novelist: A Lifetime of Lessons about Writing and Publishing*. Sourcebooks, 2008.

Needleman, Jacob. *Introduction to Tao Te Ching*, by Lao Tzu. Translated by Gia-fu Feng and Jane English. Vintage Books, 1989.

Nelson, Victoria. *On Writer's Block: A New Approach to Creativity*. Houghton Mifflin, 1993.

Nisargadatta Maharaj. *I Am That: Talks with Sri Nisargadatta Maharaj*. Translated by Maurice Frydman. Revised and edited by Sudhakar S. Dikshit. The Acorn Press, 1999. Originally published 1973.

Nouwen, Henri J. J. *Bread for the Journey: A Daybook of Wisdom and Faith*. HarperOne, 1997.

O'Connor, Flannery. *The Habit of Being: Letters of Flannery O'Connor*. Edited by Sally Fitzgerald. Farrar, Straus and Giroux, 1988.

Perry, Susan K. "How a Writer Turned One Rejection into Two Novels." Interview with Gayle Brandeis. *Psychology Today*, June 21, 2010. *https://www.psychologytoday.com/us/blog/creating-in-flow/201006/how-a-writer-turned-one-rejection-into-two-novels*.

Pressfield, Steven. "Habit." *Writing Wednesdays*, March 31, 2010. *https://stevenpressfield.com/2010/03/writing-wednesdays-32-habit*.

———. *The War of Art: Break Through the Blocks and Win Your Inner Creative Battles*. Black Irish Entertainment LLC, 2002.

Ram Dass. *Journey of Awakening: A Meditator's Guidebook*. Bantam Books, 1990.

Ramana Maharshi. *Be As You Are: The Teachings of Ramana Maharshi*. Edited by David Godman. Arkana, 1985.

———. *Talks with Ramana Maharshi*. Sri Ramanasra-mam, 2006. Originally published 1955.

———. *The Teachings of Ramana Maharshi*. Edited by Arthur Osborne. Rider Books, 2014. Originally published 1962.

Rilke, Rainer Maria. *Rilke and Andreas-Salomé: A Love Story in Letters*, translated by Edward Snow and Michael Winkler. W. W. Norton & Company, 2006.

Rogers, Carl. *On Becoming a Person: A Therapist's View of Psychotherapy*. Houghton Mifflin, 1961.

Rosenthal, A. M. "There Is No News from Auschwitz." *The New York Times*, August 31, 1958.

Samuel, William. *The Awareness of Self-Discovery*. Mountain Brook Publication Company, 1970.

Sertillanges, A. D. *The Intellectual Life: Its Spirits, Conditions, Methods*. Translated by Mary Ryan. The Newman Press, 1960.

Shapiro, Dani. "On Inspiration," June 25, 2010. *https://danishapiro.com/on-inspiration*.

Shelley, Mary. *Frankenstein; or, The Modern Prometheus*. 1818, revised in 1831.

Smith, Dean Wesley. *Writing into the Dark: How to Write a Novel without an Outline*. WMG Publishing, 2015.

Smith, Huston. *The World's Religions*. HarperSanFrancisco, 1992.

Stafford, William. *Writing the Australian Crawl*. University of Michigan Press, 1978.

Thoreau, Henry David. *Walden. In Walden, Civil Disobedience, and Other Writings*, edited by William Rossi. Library of America, 1985.

Ticknor, Art. *Solid Ground of Being*. TAT Foundation Press, 2014. Kindle.

Tolle, Eckhart. *A New Earth: Awakening to Your Life's Purpose*. Penguin Books, 2016.

———. *The Power of Now: A Guide to Spiritual Enlightenment*. New World Library, 1999.

Turak, August. *Not Less Than Everything: One Man's Quest for Spiritual Enlightenment*. Clovercroft Publishing, 2023. Kindle.

Ueland, Brenda. *If You Want to Write: A Book about Art, Independence and Spirit*. Graywolf Press, 1987. Originally published 1938.

Watts, Alan. "Alan Watts: On Being God." Talk recorded in 1971 in New York City at a conference on Western psychological therapy and Eastern religion. *Be Here Now Network*. YouTube video, 1:20:31. December 26, 2022. *https://youtu.be/sZ41zgWHs_I*.

———. *The Book: On the Taboo against Knowing Who You Are*. Pantheon Books, 1966.

Weller, Sam. *Listen to the Echoes: The Ray Bradbury Interviews*. Stop Smiling Books, 2010.

Wheeler, John. *Full Stop! The Gateway to Present Perfection*. Non-Duality Press, 2012.

———. *You Were Never Born*. Non-Duality Press, 2013.

Wilson, Robert Anton. *Right Where You Are Sitting Now: Further Tales of the Illuminati*. And/Or Press, 1982.

Wolfe, Robert. *Elementary Cloudwatching: 31 Meditations on Living without Time*. Karina Library Press, 2013.

———. *Living Nonduality*. Karina Library, 2009.

Wolff, Jurgen. "So You Don't Write Every Day? Read This!" *Time to Write*, July 8, 2010. *https://timetowrite.blogs.com/weblog/2010/07/so-you-dont-write-every-day-read-this.html*.

Wooldridge, Susan G. *Foolsgold: Making Something from Nothing and Freeing Your Creative Process*. Harmony Books, 2007.

INDEX

Aldiss, Brian 106

Angus, Kate 84–85

Apocalyptic mood 16–18, 49, 209–211, 218

Aurelius, Marcus 167, 169n5

Authentic surrender/passivity: as entry to cosmic creativity, 183–185; contrast with false quietism, 179–183; Eckhart Tolle on, 182–183

Bajani, Andrea 66–68

Berman, Morris 208–213, 215, 216. *See also* Monastic option

Bible, The 15, 29, 77, 141. *See also* Scriptures

Blackwood, Algernon 71

Bloom, Allan 158

Blue Öyster Cult 204n1

Bradbury, Ray 38, 53–55, 111, 112, 175, 205, 211

Brande, Dorothea 62, 71

Brandeis, Gayle 82–83

Buddhism 123, 127, 128

Campbell, Glen 158

Campbell, Joseph 23

Cardin, Matt: *A Course in Demonic Creativity*, 1, 10, 29, 34n1, 88n1, 131n3; journals, 118–121, 172, 173–176; *Ghosts, Spirits, and Psychics*, 119, 121; *The Living Dark* (newsletter), 37, 122, 171; *Mummies around the World*, 119, 121; piano playing and musical activities, 65–66, 129, 172; *To Rouse Leviathan*, 7, 112; *What the Daemon Said*, 29, 104, 112

Carse, David 141

Chambers, Oswald 120–121

Christianity 77

College 1–2, 41, 104, 121, 151, 156

Cope, Stephen 207–208

Creativity: accidental nature, 97–101; conscious effort vs. inspiration, 201–202; as cosmic expression, 25–26, 183–184, 184–187, 218–223; discipline and deliberate practice, 4, 28, 40, 62–64, 66–70, 78–82; embracing the unknown, 18–19, 109–113; egoic vs. authentic creativity, 47–48, 180–184, 193–199, 219–220; freewriting and morning pages, 62, 71; fulfillment through daemon muse, 215–217; as healing act, 17, 32; hidden river metaphor, 26; life as dream narrative, 25–26, 33; maze metaphor, 26; muse and daemon synergy, 26–28; paradox of personal/universal, 91–95; and personal destiny, 26, 73–74, 94, 141, 146–147, 218; relationship to spirituality, 91–92, 93–95, 133–142, 153–154; as spontaneous grace, 100–101; temptation to abandon, 117–120; transcending the creative impulse, 42; trusting the coherence of the self, 36–37; writing as waking up, 32–34; and your core question, 40–42. *See also* Daemon/daemon muse; Inspiration

Creative quietude (wu wei) 199–203, 217

Daemon/daemon muse: as ally opposing Resistance, 167–169; becoming a prepared instrument for, 68–70; as bridge to the Absolute, 148; as destiny or allotted function, 18–19; 28–31, 141, 146–147; dangers of repression and denial, 50–52; exile from Western culture, 45–52; fidelity to, 87–88; fulfillment of life purpose, 43–44, 55, 141, 146–147, 215–217; haunting and uncanny presence, 2, 70–71; as inner creative collaborator, 66–68; as inner genius or guide, 3, 17–18, 26–28; as inner other, 57–60; interplay with creativity and awakening, 141–142; as monstrous when rejected, 49–50, 54–55; moral dangers and "bad daimon," 71–74; and nonduality, 143–148, 163; recognizing presence of, 59–61, 63; relationship to ego, 3, 14, 27–28, 32, 47–48, 51–52, 59, 63, 71, 72–73, 147–148, relationship to unconscious, 32, 104–105, 148; as separate intelligence, 17, 27–28,

32, 46, 167; spectrum from constructive to destructive, 29–30; ways of divining, 60–64. *See also* Creativity; Inspiration

Daimon. See Daemon/daemon muse

Darkness (the "dark"): biblical imagery of, 15; and the daemon muse, 18; as doorway to light, 19–20; and living into the dark, 14–17; and the numinous, 18–19; as unknowable unconscious, 13–15; and the unknown, 110–111, 113, 218

DeLillo, Don 216

De Ropp, Robert S. 128–129

Ego/self: as demon, 136–138; creative drive rooted in, 141; egoic vs. authentic motivation, 193–195; illusory autonomy, 196–198; illusory nature, 147–148; relationship to Being, 197–199; as source of futility, 195–199

Emerson, Ralph Waldo 204n2

Enlightenment and scientism 46–48

Fahrenheit 451 (Bradbury) 205, 211

Ferguson, Bob 64

Flaherty, Alice 88n1

Frankenstein (Mary Shelley) 50–52, 54, 55n1, 103–106, 209

Frequency holders (Tolle) 214–215

Freud, Sigmund 47–48

Gardner, John 111–112

Goldberg, Natalie 62

Gospel of Thomas 105

Heaney, Seamus 19

Hemingway, Ernest 32

Hill, Joe 88n1

Hillman, James 73

Holiday, Ryan 167, 169n5

Horror 1, 7, 15, 38, 41, 48, 49, 53, 70–71, 105

Huston Smith 200–202

Inertia/stillness: conflict with cultural hustle, 121–122; relationship to civilization, 122; Robert Wolfe on, 122–123, 129–130; surrender to, 181–184; as temptation, 117–121; as ultimate creative state, 130

Inspiration: as accident, 97–102; biological, psychological, and/or spiritual sources, 58; as a force coming through, 2, 28, 88; disciplined vs. undisciplined approaches, 77–88; as fuel for life purpose, 214; mundane sources, 204n2; and muse/daimon, 26–27; preparedness and practice, 28, 57, 69–70; and religious scriptures, 151–153; surrender to, 27–28; waiting on, 120. *See also* Creativity; Daemon/daemon muse

Jobs, Steve 128

Joon-ho, Bong 92

Journals (Cardin) 118–121, 172–176

Jung, C. G. 23, 47, 6, 71, 158

Kierkegaard, Søren 47

King, Stephen 78, 81–82, 86

Kipling, Rudyard 66

Klein, Jean 92, 101

Language and words: breaking the spell of, 149–160; and inspiration, 69; limits of, 151–154; as pointers, not reality, 152–153; as a prison, 158–160; and silence, 127, 155–160; transmission of vision, 154–155

Lao Tzu 161

Larkin, Philip 88n1

La Ronn, Michael 9–12, 112

Ligotti, Thomas 18, 38, 71

Living into the dark 7, 12–16, 19, 110, 202, 207, 217. *See also* Writing into the dark

Lowell, Amy 88n1

Lovecraft, H. P. 38, 71, 113, 158

Maitland, Sara 134–136

Martel, J. F. 20–21n3`

McLaughlin, Mark 7

Meditation 71, 93–94, 97, 99, 135, 156–157

Monastic option: as awakened creativity, 210–214; as countercultural stance, 208–209, 211–214; creativity as fourth front, 214; and the daemon muse, 17, 215; illustrated in Bradbury's Fahrenheit 451, 211; Morris Berman on, 208–213; as orientation for life in a chaotic/collapsing culture, 4, 210–214; private preservation of wisdom, 212–213; and Tolle's "frequency holders," 214–216

Morrell, David 62

Muse. See Daemon/daemon muse

Music 43, 70, 92, 112, 157, 197

Needleman, Jacob 164, 199–200

Nelson, Victoria 38, 71, 88n1

Nietzsche, Friedrich 25, 47

Nisargadatta Maharaj 99, 199–200, 222–223

Nonduality: and awakening from separate self, 137, 138–139; and creative action in the world, 145–147; and the daemon muse, 36, 39, 143–148, 215; Jean Klein on beauty and creativity, 92; John Wheeler on, 143–145, 185–186; and the monastic option, 214–215; Ramana Maharshi on self-realization, 95; as recognition instead of philosophy, 2; Robert Wolfe on the unknown, 109; and the separate self as story, 185–187; self-realization, 36, 146–148; tension with creativity, 133–139

Nouwen, Henry 94–95

O'Connor, Flannery 78–80

Otto, Rudolf 15

Pascal, Blaise 157

Porter, Katherine Anne 78, 86

Pressfield, Steven 87, 100–101, 164–169, 181

Purpose/life purpose: beyond the mirage of ego, 195–197; found in the present moment, 192–193; as Great Work, 207–209, 215; in the marriage of action and stillness, 203; as monastic option, 208–209; as monastery of one's life, 214–218; union with Being, 217

Ram Dass 155–158, 159

Ramana Maharshi 95, 120, 205, 216, 221, 222

Religion 10–11, 52, 93, 94, 95, 128, 129, 153, 200

Resistance: capitulating to, 175–176; as deceptive egoic loop, 171–172, 176–181, 196, 198, 207, 208; and inertia, 118, 173–176; as inner enemy, 164–167; masquerading as your own thoughts, 166; opposed by inner ally, 167–169; pointing to true calling, 166–167; as ruse or con, 168–169, 181; short-circuited by authentic surrender, 181–184, 187, 202, 218. *See also* Creativity; Ego/self

Rilke, Rainer Maria 136–137, 139–140, 161

Rogers, Carl 93

Rose, Richard 99–100

Roszak, Theodore 158

Sagan, Carl 26

Samuel, William 221–222

Scriptures, religious 151–153, 155. See also Bible

Scorsese, Martin 92

Serendipity 6, 111, 168

Sertillanges, A. D. 111

Shakespeare, William 113

Shapiro, Dani 80–81

Shirley, John 204n1

Silence/stillness: authentic vs. false surrender to, 178–183; as conflict with creativity, 134–136, 139–140; as locus for hearing muse, 3–4, 31–32, 64, 65–66; more valuable than words, 127; portable inner monastery metaphor, 31–32; Ram Dass on simplicity and, 156–158; relationship to listening attention, 64–65; resting in pure being-awareness, 130; as rhythm of creativity, 77–88; surrendering to, 117–118, 121, 125–126; as threat to creativity, 133–137; as ultimate end point of creativity, 129; as ultimate teacher, 127

Sinek, Simon 5

Smith, Dean Wesley 7–10, 111

Smith, Huston 158, 200–202

Social media 32, 35–37, 122–124,

Spiritual awakening: as accidental grace, 98–100; bound up with creativity, 3, 100–101; and ego illusion, 219–220; and nonduality, 137; and self as story, 186–187; as self-remembering, 33–34, 74, 98–99; tension with creativity, 133–139, 141–142; unity with daemon and life purpose, 143–148

Spiritual teachers and traditions: Christian background of author, 77; Guardian Angel traditions, 63–64; Henri Nouwen on solitude, 94–95; Richard Rose on heaven's gates, 99; Robert Wolfe on control/unknown, 109; Zen practice and silence, 63–64, 97

Stafford, William 36, 112

Strauss, Richard 92

Suzuki, Shunryu 38

Synchronicity 7–8, 106

Taoism 98, 200–202, 217. *See also* Creative quietude

Television and film references: *Key West* (1993 television series), 124–126; *Kung Fu* (1970s television series), 126–127; *Network* (1976 film), 159–160

Thoreau, Henry David 206, 218

Ticknor, Art 127–128

Tolle, Eckhart 38, 120, 182–183, 214–215

Turak, August 99

Ueland, Brenda 62

Watts, Alan 192, 219–220

West, Rebecca 18

Wheeler, John 143–145, 185

Whitman, Walt 158

Wilson, Robert Anton 58, 75n1, 159

Wolfe, Robert 121–122, 129–130, 130–131n2, 138–139

Writing into the dark 7–12, 202. *See also* Living into the dark

Zen 26, 63, 64, 97–99, 139, 160, 203

Acknowledgments

Sᴏᴍᴇ ʙᴏᴏᴋs arrive with a long and deep cloud of debts trailing behind them. Debts of gratitude, I mean. *Writing at the Wellspring* is such a book. It is a kind of culmination for me, something I have been working toward on various levels for years. This means it's flatly impossible to remember and name everyone who contributed to its formation in one way or another. That said, some people who deserve specific mention are as follows:

J. F. Martel, Phil Ford, and Dawn Hillman of the *Weird Studies* podcast and the Weirdosphere community, not only for their enthusiasm toward my work, including the earliest draft of Wellspring, but also for their intelligence, goodwill, and friendship. Your patient, proactive interest in drawing out someone like me, who is natively prone to extended periods of introversion and withdrawal, has not, I assure you, gone unappreciated.

Everyone who signed up for the Writing at the Wellspring course in Fall 2024, which took as one of its two main texts the original manuscript version of this book. Your enthusiastic reception and insightful questions, comments, and discussions, not to mention your individual and collective kindness and intelligence, both affirmed the book's value and helped me, as its putative author, to understand it better.

The subscribers and readers of my newsletter, *The Living Dark*, where many of the essays that eventually transformed themselves into this book were first published. Your interest and support are woven into Wellspring's very existence.

D. Patrick Miller, the man behind Fearless Literary, for his excellent assistance in making a published reality out of a raw manuscript, and for guiding me through my first excursion into the world of self-publishing after many years doing it the more traditional way.

And finally, on a more abstract level, the many writers, teachers, and talismanic presences in my life whose words and insights — about creativity, about awakening, about reality, about self and cosmos, about the sheer wonder, terror, and sometimes horror of being alive and awake in this world or any other — have helped to form me. Some of you know me. Most of you don't. Many of you are named in these pages. And many of you are no longer alive, at least not in the conventional sense. As I said in the last chapter, I have always found Thoreau's famous lines about the potency of books in one's life to be vitally and immediately understandable, as if he is speaking a core truth that my whole person has been geared to receive and resonate with. All of you, the members of my intimate literary and philosophical/spiritual pantheon, have given me the experience of personal miraculous self-revelation and confirmation that I have described. You have uttered the unutterable things. When one early reader of Wellspring told me it had generated this very effect ("You got your wish, you Thoreau'd me. Words addressed to my condition exactly"), I knew the depth of what she was talking about because you gave it to me first.

To anyone I haven't named here but should have, I apologize. Perhaps the most important influences are the subterranean ones, the ones that operate at such a fundamental level that we are not even conscious of them. For those of you whose words, presence, or acts of kindness occupy that level within me, please know that I am indeed grateful, even if I'm not mindful enough to say it.

Author's Biography

M ATT CARDIN is the author of *To Rouse Leviathan* and *What the Daemon Said*, and the editor of the acclaimed two-volume reference work *Horror Literature through History*. Widely regarded as a leading interpreter of Thomas Ligotti, he co-founded *Vastarien: A Literary Journal* and has written extensively on the intersections of religion, creativity, spirituality, and the supernatural.

His work has been praised by *Publishers Weekly* and *Kirkus Reviews*, nominated for the World Fantasy Award, and long-listed for the Bram Stoker Award. A former professor of English and religion, he holds a doctorate in leadership and a master's degree in religious studies. In yet another former career, he was the live video director for pop and country music legend Glen Campbell.

Currently, he lives with his wife in the Ozarks, where he serves as a college vice president and continues to explore creativity, nonduality, and the daemon muse through *The Living Dark*, his ongoing journal of creative and spiritual inquiry.

ALSO BY MATT CARDIN

FICTION

Divinations of the Deep
Dark Awakenings (stories and essays)
To Rouse Leviathan

NONFICTION

A Course in Demonic Creativity: A Writer's Guide to the Inner Genius
What the Daemon Said: Essays on Horror Fiction, Film, and Philosophy
Journals, Volume 1: 1993–2001
Journals, Volune 2: 2002–2022
Writing at the Wellspring

AS EDITOR

Born to Fear: Interviews with Thomas Ligotti
Mummies around the World: An Encyclopedia of Mummies in History,
    Religion, and Popular Culture
Ghosts, Spirits, and Psychics: The Paranormal from Alchemy to Zombies
Horror Literature through History (two volumes)